*Joanne & Bob,*
*For the angling wing of your library – hope you enjoy it.*
*Love, John*
*12/17/97*

# Stripers

## An Angler's Anthology

John Waldman, Editor

Foreword by John Cole

RAGGED MOUNTAIN PRESS
Camden, Maine

# International Marine/
# Ragged Mountain Press

A Division of The **McGraw·Hill** Companies

10   9   8   7   6   5   4   3   2   1

*Library of Congress Cataloging-in-Publication Data*

Stripers : an angler's anthology / John Waldman, editor.
    p.   cm.
  Includes bibliographical references.
  ISBN 0-07-067810-3
  1. Striped bass fishing.    I. Waldman, John R.
  SH691.S7S77 : 1997                       97-19656
  799.1 '7732—DC21                          CIP

Questions regarding the content of this book should be addressed to:

Ragged Mountain Press
P.O. Box 220
Camden, ME 04843

Questions regarding the ordering of this book should be addressed to :

The McGraw-Hill Companies
Customer Service Department
P.O. Box 547
Blacklick, OH 43004
Retail customers: 1-800-262-4729
Bookstores: 1-800-233-4726

A portion of the profits from the sale of each Ragged Mountain Press book is donated to an environmental cause.

*Stripers* is printed on 60-pound Renew Opaque Vellum, an acid-free paper containing 50 percent recycled waste paper (preconsumer) and 10 percent postconsumer waste paper.

Illustrated by Stephen Hensel
Printed by R.R. Donnelley
Design and Production by University Graphics, Inc., York, PA

Permissions information can be found in the Bibliography.

For Carol, my safe harbor.

For the gifts of life are the earth's
and they are given to all,
and they are the songs of birds at daybreak,
Orion and the Bear,
and dawn seen over ocean from the beach.

—HENRY BESTON, *The Outermost House,* 1928

# Contents

# Foreword

by John Cole

"T|he way to catch them is with hook and line, the fisherman taking a great cod line to which he fasteneth a peece of lobster and threwes it into the sea. The fish biting at it, he pulls her to him and knocks her on the head with a sticke."

These succinct instructions for striped bass anglers by William Wood appeared in a slim volume entitled "New England's Prospect," published in 1634, more than 150 years before George Washington was sworn in as our nation's first president.

A century after Washington, an ingenious public servant named Harry W. Mason spent ten days working with a haul seine crew on the Navesink River in Red Bank, New Jersey. Of the 167 striped bass that he shipped in tanks aboard a transcontinental boxcar, 107 survived and were released in the Carquinez Straits near San Francisco. Twenty years later, the West Coast commercial striped bass catch topped one million pounds.

There is no fish more American than the striper. It swims from sea to shining sea. Riding a moon tide's elemental surge, these gleaming bronze and silver creatures cruise our innermost salt marsh creeks, sliding silently beneath a great oak's dark shadow as they glide by farm fields of salt hay. Thrusting the length of the Hudson, striper schools flash bright just beyond Albany's grimy streets.

These splendid creatures are masters of all manner of marine environments. From Maine's easternmost St. John River to Montauk's merciless surf, off the nubbled ledges of Cape Cod and Jersey's sweeping sand beaches, in the gloom of Virginia's James River, the striper swims for all.

It abides all manner of desire. For landlocked anglers, the striper swims among submerged cottonwood stumps in artifical Texas lakes. Surprised spin casters sometimes hook them in tidal creeks all along the Gulf of Mexico.

For this is a fish of vast generosity, offering itself as sport and sustenance to the many tens of millions of Americans who live within a day's drive of the coast. The striper does not stint, not one bit. It is there for the adolescent with his or her first rod and reel. It waits for the anglers who earn wages from nine to five and then sacrifice their sleep to pursue dreams of great stripers hovering in moon-tossed surf. Stripers are strung like pearls across turbulent tides where trolled lures hang like tinsel strung by stubbled men and shirted women seeking surcease from cities in the sterns of open boats.

The fish is there for the solitary angler walking dawn's edge along a salt marsh silvered with winding creeks, just as it is there for the urban fisher at the river's rim, mere steps from traffic's thunder and chaos. This is a fish determined not to disappoint.

From one pound to one hundred, the stripers are there. From Maine to California, they are there. Indeed, they commit to coastal waters. It is their pledge never to stray offshore. They make themselves available, year-round if you know where to look. They belong to all. They are everyone's fish, without artifice, without snobbery, without implications of aristocracy. For although they are noble—in the word's best sense—they are also the essence of democracy.

Which does not imply they are easy. No, not by a long shot. Fascinating, yes, but not easy. Stripers are courageous, generous, pugnacious—but never easy. If you doubt this, turn to almost any of the following pages in this sweeping collection of striper encounters. You will learn of submersion and drowning. You will discover new dimensions of discomfort as well as pages strewn with broken hopes and ravaged tackle. There are thousands of dark days and darker nights, along with collective decades of fruitless striper fishing.

For even though the striped bass are there waiting, they are never easy. So what you have is this captivating creature: exquisite, strong, large, powerful, wild and yet available to those who make the effort and the sacrifice to learn to know it. And *there* is the striper's ultimate paradox. Because by the time the striper has taught you what you need to know, you have so come to love this greatest of American game fishes that you can only wish it well. Godspeed! you say as you set free what once you most wanted to possess.

Ah, but for all of us, there is this book to keep.

# Preface

S| triped bass swam into my consciousness one summer night
early in my boyhood. My dad, who rarely fished for stripers, had
spent the day trolling sandworms around Long Island Sound's
bedrock shoals. The effort resulted in one, barely legal-sized schoolie.
Until then, I had been only vaguely aware of this eminent gamefish.
But when I saw the little striper on my kitchen counter, I knew I was
viewing another echelon in angling—far above my familiar league of
sunfish and flounder—and I sensed this fish was the emblem of a
path to be followed. I handled that bass for a very long time, examin-
ing its every scale, tooth, and fin ray; lifeless, stripes since faded, its
presence nonetheless was captivating, and I felt compelled to know
the striped bass better.

Since then the fish has brought me much pleasure—both mo-
mentary and ongoing—in a great diversity of settings.

As an angler and outdoorsman, I have stood in a crowd on a brilliant autumn day and viewed pods of striped bass herding baitfish
along the beach, and then waded seaward to a boulder to watch a
school of bass sweep through the knee-high shallows where I had
walked moments earlier, the fish's fins erect and stripes vivid as they
gave rapid chase.

Alone, I have fumbled along cliffside trails beneath a new moon
sky, pausing to rest from hours spent arching plugs far out over the

breakers, body fatigued but spirit uplifted, aspirations of the night fully rewarded by battle with more than a dozen stripers in the wash of a rock-strewn reef—to stand under a million stars and listen to the ocean far below.

I have snorkeled in the rush of a clear river and watched bright striped bass fight the flow in the company of smallmouth bass and other riverine fishes; farther upstream, I have taken on the fly stripers mixed with bluegills in a most trout-like setting.

Balancing on a stone at night in a heavy surf, I have been repeatedly knocked off my stand, only to climb back to cast again into the ripcurrent, confident the fish should be there, and then finally connecting with a large striper, leaning against the weight of the fish, satisfied—maybe vindicated—as the rod bucked and the reel's drag yielded to the fish's first run. And I have slipped into the placid evening waters of a tidal marsh to toss and strip a streamer fly, the striper's strikes imparting that sweet, direct, and utterly tactile yank offered only by the primitive dropline and the graceful fly rod.

I have caught striped bass in the dazzling cityscape of New York Harbor—near the Statue of Liberty and the United Nations building, in the boiling waters of Hell Gate—and even to the applause of the port-side passengers on the Staten Island Ferry. I have fished in a flooding southern river, landing dozens of stripers or "rock" holding behind submerged trees in the roily brown water. And I have plugged for stripers in a pristine Canadian estuary with tides so immoderate that each succeeding wave on the ebb broke farther down the bank than the one before it.

I have greeted each spring and said farewell to too many autumns with my waders on, seeking stripers, and in between, the season long, found both recreation and refuge in the myriad stations where striped bass are found. And while on the water, I have met some of the most dedicated and idiosyncratic anglers to be found in the sport.

As a father, I have brought my children to the sea where they have learned to watch gulls and terns for signs of stripers; the fishing only a small part of their enchantment with the shore.

As a scientist, I have traveled, collecting striped bass for study from many of the great tidal rivers where they spawn, and gathering them from the ocean surf with baymen who practice the waning but anachronistically beautiful art of haul seining. It has been an intellectual privilege to decipher the biology of this always surprising species—tagging stripers to learn where they wander, flushing their stomachs before releasing them to know what they consume, and to distinguish their populations, counting their fin rays and scales and mixing exotic chemicals to reveal information locked in their genes. I have even fed striped bass to insect colonies to bare their bones, using the still-articulated skeletons to deduce the striper's evolutionary affinities.

And as an infatuate of striped bass, I have read all that I could find on the fish. The literature on angling for stripers, unlike that on the also-revered trouts, is enormously biased toward the how, not the why. Assembly of this anthology required spending considerable time casting about in libraries and antiquarian book shops—pleasurable angling of a different sort.

Fortunately, Cole, Chatham, Bryant, and others smitten with the species have produced sufficient devotional writing to constitute this collection. Authors normally not associated with angling, such as Boyle and Frazier, also contributed their impressions of the striper world. The chapters have been arranged to flow loosely in a seasonal arc, reflecting the annual cycle's mounting spring run; its peak, climactic experiences; and denouement. Certain themes resonate throughout: the sheer comeliness of the fish; the splendor and mystery of the sea; darkness and dawn; the angler's early or sudden captivation with striped bass followed by frustration, hard lessons, and finally, a felicitous success; pride in the mastery of necessary, highly specialized skills; the excitement of seabirds wheeling and fish swirling in a blitz; the incongruities and special circumstances of urban striper fishing; camaraderie or ablutionary solitude, as sought; an openness and sense of wonder toward the natural world; and a passion for the adventure the sport so readily affords.

Compilation of this volume was a labor of love; its product, a celebration of stripers.

The International Game Fish Association and the Franklin B. Lord Collection of Long Island University were sources for much of the older material in this anthology. Robert Boyle, Nick Lyons, and George Reiger suggested fine works on stripers I had not encountered. Thanks also to Clay Hiles, my ever-encouraging wordsmith-at-call; to my children, Steven and Laura; and to Steve Gabriel, Felix Locicero, Dave Taft, and Ike Wirgin, all of whom have shared many a tide with me seeking the intractable linesiders.

# 1

# Spring Migration

### John Cole

N o better tribute to the striped bass has been written than John Cole's heartfelt work, Striper: A Story of Fish and Man (1978). In these passages, Cole provides a lyrical introduction to the characteristics of stripers and a description of their annual exodus from Chesapeake Bay—a migration that is an integral component of the great stream of life that vitalizes northern waters in springtime.

---

Men can not become fish, nor can fish transform themselves into men. But over the centuries, men have learned to appreciate in creatures, qualities that are also recognizable in humans. Men who know the striper know it to be a creature of strength and sinew, endowed with a unique determination to survive. Few other fish will attempt the striper's runs and lunges; none have attained the striper's mastery of the surf and the tides—those turbulent inshore presences which other fish avoid, and in which the striper is most itself. Like shafts of muscular light, the striped bass races through the arcs of breaking waves, swirls in the white water of rolling surf, rolls in the tumult of a riptide, somehow finding the power in its broad tail and bronze shoulders to master currents that no other creature can navigate.

If there is a reason for this, the same men who say the striper is courageous and vital also explain that these qualities are the heritage of its dangerous beginnings. From the days of its genesis in the darkness of the swirling Nanticoke, out of the murk of millions of its brothers' drifting skeletons, from the terror of the first hunt, its earliest killings, and the attacks of other predators upon it, the surviving striper emerges with a sinewed heart, a vast capacity for courage, a determined will to live. Having endured so much of the nearness of death, the creature generates an extraordinary exuberance for life.

To have survived, to have endured winter ice, the suffocation of summer's heat, to have somehow avoided the deaths that scattered like grain from a torn sack, these are the searing experiences that provide the pulse to the broad bass tails. From each of the risks run and dangers cleared, has come a full measure of life force—an appreciation of existence that gives these animals the strength to swim, leap, roll, and lunge with a degree of pure energy that surpasses most others.

Riding the river currents to the sea, they will travel south to Cape Charles where the bay meets the open ocean. From there, the stripers will turn north, creatures of the wild Atlantic now, embarking on an adventure which began on an April night more than fifty miles north in the Nanticoke's milky swirls of milt.

No, there is no way the fare charged the striper for its annual trips can ever be computed. Every fish taken becomes a river of fish, then a cataract of billions, cascading over the centuries in a torrent of silver shapes that roars its testimony to nature's awesome abundance.

In their annual verification of that abundance, mature stripers still leave the rivers around the Chesapeake every spring after they have spawned. Thinned and weakened by the vigor and intensity of their spawning, the fish ease down the rivers, borne as much by the current as by the listless movement of their tails. After the April nights when the rivers gleam with the fecundity of these fish, the stripers depart the Nanticoke, the Choptank, the Wicomico, the

Chester, the Pocomoke, the Wye, the Corsica, the Sassafras and four-teen more Chesapeake rivers that are still striper nurseries. On their way, the spent fish are taken by the river's drift netters, but once by those and in the open bay, they are relatively free of harassment by fishermen.

Starved during their spawning, the fish feed as they travel, gath-ering numbers as they move, segregating into schools according to size and age, establishing the behavior patterns that will set the schools on a compass course—first south to the bay's gateway at Cape Charles, then north along the barrier beaches of Maryland, past the oil refineries and chemical plants of Delaware and New Jersey, then across Sandy Hook and the Hudson delta in the shadow of the Statue of Liberty, and then past Brooklyn, Coney Island, Fire Island and on along the edge of the open Atlantic to the beaches of eastern Long Island and the oceanic migratory crossroads at Montauk Point where the Atlantic meets Long Island Sound and Block Island Sound and where twenty or more species of food fish and game fish gather during the year on their migratory travels. Of these comings and go-ings, none is more certain, more regular than the arrival of the striped bass in May.

Movement ripples through Long Island's temperate spring on land and in the air as well as under the sea. Furred, hibernating crea-tures of the woods emerge from their dens; geese, warblers, wildfowl, shorebirds and the redwing blackbird flock to the marshes and thick-ets of this sandy, scrub oak plain. This wind-scoured island has somehow withstood enough of the pressures of the city's millions to still provide East End ponds where Canada geese can rest on their flight from Carolina to Labrador, or where the golden plover can swing down for a safe pause on their three-thousand-mile trans-national trip from South America.

There are great spring floods of fish, undersea rivers that over-flow their banks. First the herring, the alewives, bluebacks, and bunkers, the dense fluttering pods of their millions darkening the waters like oval clouds of blue dye, their nervous, fragile tails stip-pling the sea's surface like a squally breeze, the sound of their placid progress hissing gently like the wake of a sailing ship.

And after the herring come the dogfish, toothless cousins to the shark—summer dog and spiny dog, gray replicas of shark shapes, but in such numbers that if ever they should sprout the teeth and meanness of sharks there would soon be no other fish in the sea. They glide by Long Island's eastern beaches in May, the bellies of the females stretched with their cargoes of pups, the infant dogfish born complete, dropped swimming by the dozen from their mothers' wombs with a day's supply of food suspended in the yolk at their umbilici—a day, that's all, to learn to hunt, catch and eat.

Under the dogs move skates and rays, flying over the sea bottom on the undulating wings that give such grace to these creatures of whipping tails and ugly, grimacing features set in the pale alabaster of their unseen undersides. And with the rays and skates, nuzzling the same sea floor, are the sea robins, sand crabs, lady crabs, blue-claw crabs, spider crabs, angler fish, scup, sea bass, tautog, ling, sturgeon, and starfish—all of these and more setting the sea in motion with the sustained movements of their May migration.

The inshore Atlantic, the half-mile of breaking, rolling, surging sea between the outer sand bar fashioned by the largest swells and the inner, barrier beach where the land begins, here in this single ribbon of brine, the scale of life becomes overwhelming in the Long Island spring. From the quiet windless dawns to the evenings ruffled by the afternoon's southwest winds, the corridor teems. Small bait fish—the silver-sided spearing and the sardine-sized herring—flash like a silver rain blown from under the sea. Terrified by the approach of an infant dogfish, or panicked by a scup's rush, the dense schools of these finger-length mites take to the air as if they could find safety where they can not breathe.

When the bait schools shatter the surface and spray upwards in the sun they make a sound like the tearing of a cotton sheet. If the feeding fish are persistent, terns and gulls gather screaming in the sky. Then, as the hapless minnows leap from the yawning mouths below, they jump into the scissoring beaks above. But it takes a feeding frenzy to alert entire flocks of birds. More often, the silver showers of bait break here, there, the length of the beach in occasional and random patterns little noted by either bird or human, yet which are overall a daily and nightly part of the spring sea's particular pattern.

It is only when the stripers and the other school fish move that the birds are likely to gather. First come the small bass, then the middle-weights, and finally, the ponderous patriarchs and matriarchs, the thirty, forty, fifty, and sixty pound fish who wait until May is almost gone before they slide past Shinnecock and the Hamptons. With them come the weakfish, bluefish and some of the larger sharks—makos, threshers and hammerheads.

There is an order to the procession. Places are made for all, even the dense and apparently aimless schools of blowfish, packing stupidly just behind the surf even though the conformation of their stubby frames and inadequate tails makes it difficult for them to survive the inshore surging. Somehow they do survive, even though breaking swells are often darkened by cargoes of hundreds of the small creatures tossed in disarray by their own misjudgments.

The bass make no such errors; nor do the blues and weakfish— the primary school, toothed, muscular feeders of the inshore territory. These are the mass killers of the silverside, the mullet, the herring, the shrimp, the tinker mackerel, the blueback and the bunker. When a school of three hundred or four hundred stripers receives its simultaneous feeding message from impulses not yet fully deciphered by humankind, the creatures detonate a group frenzy that shatters the water's surface with the violence of an erupting undersea geyser.

Everywhere the bait fish fly, as if some soundless, invisible tornado were sucking them up from beneath the sea. Broad bass tails smash the surface in white welts of foam; the turnings of the feeding fish start scores of swirling whirlpools, each a mark of the consummate energy a fish needs to reverse its course and swerve open-mouthed through the very center of the mass of panic the bait fish school has become. Shredded bits of bunker, spearing or blueback drift to a surface made slick with the released oils of the tiny, dismembered fish. Sea birds scream of the carnage; their coarse signals carry for miles, attracting hundreds, sometimes thousands of their kin. Then the air above becomes part of the tumultuous mass—a sky filled with stripped feathers, the hysterical cry of anxious terns, the hoarser calls of the herring and blackback gulls, all diving, wheeling, hovering and heedless of any approach as they swallow the hapless bait fish whole whenever the prey are driven live from the sea, or pick with their bills at the flesh fragments that rise in the wake of the stripers' feeding rush.

The gluttony ends with the same unity it began. Another coded message stills the sated school, the birds become silent, scatter; just a few stay sitting on the surface, drifting markers on a patch of sea, mobile memorials to the oceanic moment when ten thousand tiny herring were devoured.

The striper school moves on, traveling east to Montauk, guided by the sound of the rolling surf, compelled to continue by voices calling across the Ice Age with urgings that have transcended every fear of net, spear, hook, and trap since the bass first embarked on their journey, before the Indians, before the colonists, . . . and before Manhattan's millions.

# Fishing in American Waters

*Genio Scott*

 enio Scott, *author of* Fishing in American Waters *(1869), was an early champion of the striped bass as a sportfish. Two passages from this work are placed around New York City—perhaps the center of American saltwater angling in the mid-1800's. The first describes lively action with striped bass in the then bucolic Harlem River, at that time a resort area at the outskirts of the city. The second passage is an account of fishing in the East River at Hell Gate—a boiling rip through a reef-strewn channel famous both for its frequent ship wrecks and its striper fishing. The third passage, a dialogue between Scott and a visiting doctor, takes place at a New England bassing club. These organizations provided ritualized sport for gentlemen who cast off "bass stands" elevated above the rocky surf and who employed "ghillies" to chum and gaff the fish—a long gone, but colorful phase in the grand tradition of striper fishing.*

---

As the fishes of the Atlantic coast of North America, including those of the estuaries and tidal waters which debouch along our coast, are more numerous, and include a greater variety for both the angler and the commercial fisherman than do the finny tribes of the coasts of any other country, and as nearly every American angler of a tidal river regards the striped bass as the fish of fishes *par excellence* to be angled for, I trust that I shall be pardoned for placing this beauty first on the list, and showing some of the artistic ways for taking him.

This fish, so beautiful and gamesome, is peculiar to the tidal waters and estuaries of the rivers which empty on the coast of the Atlantic from Portland to Norfolk. The striped bass is known farther north and south, but it exists in the most perfect state in the rivers and along the coast between the points named. It affords good sport with light tackle when its weight is but half a pound; and it tries both the mettle and skill of an angler after it rises to the ponderous importance of ten pounds, though it is said to attain to the weight of nearly a hundred. I have captured but one which weighed over forty pounds, although I have angled for them every season for the past thirty years. It is great game when weighing anywhere from ten to thirty pounds. In muscular power the striped bass equals the salmon, but it lacks the caudal power for leaping, which is so palpable in the form of a salmon, back of its adipose fin, including its crescent-shaped tail.

This fish is known south of New Jersey as the rockfish; but as no two ichthyologists agree upon a classical name for the fish, it had probably best be called the name by which it is known where the greatest numbers are taken, and there it is known only as the *striped bass*; and as there is no other fish which at all resembles it, there is no chance of mistake. It approximates the *Perca genus,* the front dorsal fin being composed of seven spinous or spiked rays, and having two nearly concealed spines. Its scales are rather large, and of metallic lustre; gill-covers serrated and edges sharp. The color of the back is a blending of black, blue, and green, lightening to bluish-gray at the sides, and to a satin white belly. The longitudinal stripes are usually seven or eight in number, and are like narrow black braids, sparkling with silver or diamonds and emerald. Its symmetry, marks, and satin sheen render it one of the most picturesque and interesting fishes in the world, independent of its great game, generous play, and luxury as a dinner fish.

The striped bass is eminently domestic in his habits. He is not given to wandering or vagrancy. He is generally to be found at home and in good condition. The female deposits her eggs in fresh and brackish waters, but never in the sea. In November the bass shoal and congregate in brackish water-ponds, or back waters of tidal rivers, or in the bays and bayous of rivers which have an outlet to the sea, after which time it will not take bait until the following spring, after having spawned and returned to active waters. The ponds formed by the backwater of the Seconnet River were, a few winters since, so full of striped bass that the fish were discovered by their dorsal fins in the ice, where they had been frozen by too close packing. The ice was cut, and hundreds of cart-loads were pitched out with forks and taken to market.

Striped bass will live and increase when confined to fresh water, but its shape then becomes changed, and instead of its symmetry and lustre when having access to both fresh and salt waters, it becomes more chubbed, and its colors less scintillant. This I discovered in those I took in the upper part of Lake Ontario, and it corroborates the opinion which I have heard expressed by other anglers and fish-culturists.

These fish delight in rocky shoals, among which they flap their tails and rub their scales as they prospect for *crustacea,* of which shedder and soft-shell crabs they consider great delicacies. Their great power and swiftness enable them to forage with impunity for disabled menhaden, spearing, shrimp, crabs, shedder lobsters, etc., among the breakers, as they lash and lave the rocky shores of our coast; and it is at such times, when the sea is agitated, that casting for them from the rocks with rod, and reel, and menhaden bait, that the sport is rendered more pleasingly exciting and attractive than angling for any other game fish.

Angling for Striped Bass

In order that the reader may proximately realize the character of the striped bass as a game fish, I propose taking him with me on several excursions after the lustrous beauty. And, first, we will try him in the vicinity of New York. The weather and tide are favorable, and the moon is right for giving fish an excellent appetite and great activity. Fishes in waters near the ocean bite best in the first quarter of the moon, while those which are up rivers and creeks, near fresh water, bite best at full tides, and immediately after a "nor'easter," when the wind, having backed round by the south has settled in the northwest. You may prove these facts without going a dozen miles from the metropolis; and I have always noticed that it is better fishing in "the Kills" and at the hedges of Newark Bay, as well as at those in the lower part of the Bay of New York, when the tide is low, while the fishing at King's Bridge and Spuyten Duyvel is best at very high tides. The only exception to this rule is applicable to reefs and low rocky shoals, where bass forage most during high tides.

As we are to try the bass to-morrow, suppose we make a day of it? Well, that being agreed to, we will first try Harlem River, or the creek at King's Bridge. Being an angler, you of course know that the baits here are confined to shrimp early in spring and late in autumn; to soft-shell and shedder crab in the summer and until the middle of October; after which soft-shell clam for the English Neighborhood Bridge, and shrimp, with an occasional shedder lobster, serve as baits in the vicinity of New York, except for trolling in Hell Gate, where we use squid; and for fishing in the surf at Newport, and along the coast generally, the menhaden is preferred.

Well, brother angler, a night of sound sleep, and our incomparable breakfast at the Astor, with our drive over the Bloomingdale Road this beautiful morning, has so enlivened me to a sense of the beautiful that I feel assured we shall have good sport to-day, and enjoy it. This is King's Bridge, the name of the most spicy and succulent oyster that ever graced the *cuisine* of a Dorlon. Our horse will be well cared for at this hotel, for the host—an admirable caterer—appreciates anglers.

We will first see what sport there is to be had at the east bridge, where we will joint our rods, and rig sinkers and floats according to the movement of the tide. I perceive that the tide is just on the turn to flood. Rig light for half an hour, and then change to heavier sinker and larger float. I like bridge fishing, for, after making a cast, you may humor your line so as to lead the bait in the most angling manner from current to current; and then, in striking at a bite forty yards off, there is so much sport in playing your fish until you get him into the slack water formed by the piers of the bridge; and, being from 8 to 10 feet above the water, you generally fasten the fish at the first bite. Strike! You've hooked him! There!

Give him play, but feel his weight, and make him contend for every foot of line you give him, or he will take the whole without exhausting himself, and you will lose him. Do not permit him to run back on you, for that is a favorite dodge of these striped sides to get slack line, and enable them to dislodge the hook. Keep your rod up nearly perpendicular, giving him the benefit of its spring, for he is bony-mouthed, though the teeth in his upper jaw are too small and short to bite or even chafe off a silk-worm gut snell. Keep your fish out of the swiftest of the tide, and, after playing him until he succumbs from exhaustion, land him on the shore, for he is too heavy to lift upon the bridge. Well done! Now bait quickly and cast for another. You perceive that at the foot of the rapid tide the bass lie in wait for bait, for our floats dip at that place. But the fish move away from there after the tide gets running its full strength, and an hour is all of first-rate fishing we may expect in one tide, therefore it is necessary to be active in baiting and expert at casting and playing a fish, always using shrimp on the upper hook and shedder on the lower one, when you use two baits at a time in this style of fishing. Now, as the tide has become too swift for float-fishing, just step into this boat, and we will row down to the first island in the creek, seventy-five rods beyond the west bridge, and try Spuyten Duyvel Creek. The fish are smaller here, but they bite more generously. I took 174 here in one day, and yet Judge Brevoort, my companion, beat me by one fish. See! one on each hook at every cast! Say you not that angling for small bass with light tackle forms a pleasing excitement? Well, having fished out the tide, suppose we return to the hotel and take our vehicle for home? This place is accessible by public conveyances over several routes, but as it is only eleven miles from the City Hall, I prefer to drive out. We have taken between thirty and forty bass which scale from half a pound to a pound each—only three two-pound fish and one three-pounder; and this may be regarded as an average morning's sport.


Trolling in Hell Gate

Now for the fray! Our boats are made by Hughes, fellow apprentice of George Steers; and with Sile Wright and Sandy Gibson as guides and gaffers, we shall be sculled over all the favorite trolling grounds from the ferry below to the Drowned Marsh above Ward's Island. Our first move will be toward Tide Rock, swinging Big and Little Mill Rocks on the way; then we shall glide over the Hen and Chickens, swing Holt's Rock on the Hog's Back, round Nigger Point, and, stopping at John Hilliker's to rest, enjoy a piece of incomparable apple-pie and a glass of milk served by two charming ladies. While indulging these ruminations one day, as my friend was swinging* Holt's Rock, he hooked a large bass and played it all the way round the east end of Ward's Island to Chowder Eddy, where, on landing, it weighed twenty pounds.

I was not so fortunate as my friend; for, as my squid was struck by a large bass, Sile said he heard the rod crack; but the fish made such a long, vigorous run, that I scarcely realized what he said, and, after turning the fish and reeling him in gradually, he broke water with a leap, clearing the surface, and revealing a forty-pounder. While turning and bringing him toward the boat for the third time, he darted down and snapped the middle joint of my rod in two, when I threw the broken rod down at my feet and took hold of the line; the fish made but feeble resistance, and I towed him alongside the boat and shouted to Sile for the gaff, but he had thoughtlessly placed it in the other boat. I then endeavored to put my hand in his mouth, and, while in the act, the fish turned over, breaking the hook and bleeding profusely as he settled off into the tide, leaving us astonished and almost desperate. On examination, I learned that a flaw in the hook had been the cause of our loss of the fish; but had we rowed ashore and towed the fish after the rod broke, we should probably have landed him.

---

*Swinging a rock is done by the oarsman holding the boat sixty feet from the rock and swinging it so that the troll will move about the rock on all sides and play as if alive. This art is possessed in great perfection by Hell Gate oarsmen.

Well, with broken rod and tangled line, I ordered Sile to row away from the scene of our misfortune, I found my friend at Hammock Rocks, his fish laid out in state on rock-grass, and he mutely bending over it with a face radiant with pleasurable satisfaction at his achievement. Trolling, to him, was a new-born pleasure, and his first capture a trophy of which a slayer of lions might be justly proud. It would be superfluous to add, we drank to the study for a Stearns or a Bracket as it lay shining on the pallet of sea-grass. Sandy commiserated Sile's misfortune at losing the large bass. In the centre of a radius containing the most picturesque landscape near the metropolis, we rested, wondered, and admired.

"The skies their fairest canvas spread
When the angler goes a-trolling;
Relenting clouds float overhead,
And tears and smiles alternate shed,
When the angler goes a-trolling."—STODDART

Having toasted the health and appetite of bass in that neighborhood in a glass of sherry, and replaced the broken joint of my rod with a sound one, we again seated ourselves in our boats, and commenced trolling the Little Gate, the Kills, and all about Randall's and Ward's Islands, and, after the usual alternatives of hopes, fears, and moments of ecstasy, we finished up a mess of seven bass between us, the largest nearly thirty, and the smallest four pounds in weight.

### Casting Bait for Striped Bass

Casting menhaden bait for striped bass from the rocky shores of the bays, estuaries, and islands along the Atlantic coast constitutes the highest branch of American angling. It is indeed questionable—when considering all the elements which contribute toward the sum total of sport in angling—whether this method of striped bass fishing is not superior to fly-fishing for salmon, and if so, it outranks any angling in the world. The method is eminently American, and characteristic of the modern angler by its energy of style, and the exercise and activity necessary to success.

*A Day with the Doctor—Angling at the Bassing Clubs*

Well, doctor, having arrived at West Island, which is owned by an association of gentlemen who have formed themselves into a club for the incomparable enjoyment of angling for striped bass, they will of course assign us stands to fish from to-morrow. It is the practice here for all members to draw at night for the choice of stands to fish from the next day.

*Doctor.* A gentleman just handed me a card containing a "number," and "outside the Hopper," marked on it.

*S.* I perceive by the card that the outside of the Hopper is assigned to us. Well, if course that is owing to the composition of the club; the members have given us their best stands. That is a feature of all the bassing clubs; and besides, William C. Barrett, Esq., is president of this institution, and he is a sportsman possessed of the most discriminative sense of true hospitality. On the morrow we will try to do honor to their estimate of us.

*D.* Gentlemen, as Mr. S. and myself are somewhat fatigued, and would prefer to retire early, will you have the goodness to join us in a parting glass for the night?

All join; and we retire with a sense of good-will toward all mankind, and indulge school-boy hopes of the morrow.

> "While others are brawling, let anglers agree,
> And in concord the goblet replenish;
> 'Twill cost not a care so long as we share
> The cups of content and of concord."

Our dreams were rose-tinted; but the pleasurable anticipations of the morrow's exploits caused us to awake early, and I sounded the doctor before daylight.

*S.*   Hallo, doctor! Mosier, who is to be our gaffer, rapped at my door and said it was four o'clock.

*D.*   Well, sir, I have been up an hour, and down on the piazza trying to joint my rod, but I can not get a light, and "daylight don't appear."

*S.*   Bravo! I'll be with you in a minute.

*D.*   The sea fog sets in chilly; what say you to a cocktail and a cracker?

*S.*   Oh! Do you know where we are?

*D.*   Certainly; we are near Plymouth Rock, the blarney-stone of America.

*S.*   Tush! I will accompany you, and we will take a stomachic and a cracker; but do not—for appearance sake—call drinks by their ordinary names in this "land of steady habits," where it is unlawful to taste diffusible stimulants.

*D.*   For medicine?

*S.*   Of course not, if prescribed by a physician!

*D.*   It was upon that hypothesis I ventured the invitation. I brought my diploma with me, and, as a doctor, I prescribe the potion.

*S.*   Ahem! you are right; I feel that your prescription is a good antarthritic. And now we will hie to the Hopper Rocks, take our stands, joint our rods, and be ready by the time Mosier gets the fish chummed in. Mosier calls up the bass here just as a framer brings his chickens to feed. Let us prepare; but there is no use to make a cast before sunrise.

*Mosier.*   I've throwed in the chum of six fish, an them scups an cachockset comes up an takes it just for all the world as if they was game! an I hain't seen nothin of no bass yet.

*S.*   That is right, doctor! you have jointed your rod perfectly; every joint should be driven home. Now, in fastening the hook to your line, cast two half hitches with the end of your line over the shank, just below the head; then turn up the end of the line, and cast a half hitch over it and the shank, and turn the hook round in the tie thus formed to see that it revolves easily—cut off any superfluous end of line. See how Mosier chops up the chum, and where he throws it; and just where he throws the chum, cast your baited hook. Mosier, bait the doctor's hook. I see luminous rays from the God of Day, and he will make a splendid appearance in ten minutes. Now, doctor, reel up your line, so that the bait will be within a yard of the top of your rod, and make a cast to the whirl which you see was made by a bass. Your reel overruns? That is unfortunate. You should keep your thumb on the reel, and check it as the bait drops on the water. Mosier, bait my hook; I have put on a medium-sized hook with a headed shank, and I am going in for the fish refused by the doctor.

*Mosier.* Mr. S. jist cast along there in Snecker's Gap, for they are reether sassy there on the young flood.

*S.* Well, Mosier, here goes for a forty-pounder!

*Mosier.* There! I told you so; I knew that feller wanted breakfast, an I guess he's got enough to last him.

*D.* Mr. Mosier, as I have succeeded in getting my line out of snarl, shall I cast now?

*Mosier.* Not quite yet, I guess, for there's no knowin where that critter will yet lead Mr. S.

*D.* Well, I will take a seat on the rock here, and look at the play. Ugh! that wave wet me all over. Is it not dangerous to remain here?

*Mosier.* No, sir; ony keep a look-out for them ninth waves; don't git down toward a gulch, but watch where the waves throw the most water when they break, for it allers depends on the course of wind.

*D.* I see your philosophy is correct, Mr. Mosier, and I have now got a dry seat. Mr. Mosier, do you think that fish will ever be landed? He has run nearly all the line off the reel already.

*Mosier.* I can't say; there's no counting on them chaps till they are landed, if so be you fish with a pole; but if I had him on my hand-line, I'd make him come humming, and show no quarters.

*S.*   Mosier, keep my line away from the rocks with your gaff, for he seems bent on rounding the Hopper Rock, and its corners may cut or chafe and part my line. There! he has tacked again; be ready to gaff him, if I get him near enough, before he makes another run.

*Mosier.*   I see his mate a keeping alongside of him all the time; she's 'bout as big as the hooked one. I mean to gaff that one first. How like tarnation the feller fights, an tries to whip out the hook with his tail; that shows he's gitting tired. When they curl themselves up on the top of the water so that you can't budge 'em, you had better be careful not to hold so hard as to let 'em break the line with their tail, nor cut it off with their back fin; nor so loose as to let him git slack line to unhook, or knock the hook out of his jaw with his tail. There! see him straighten out! He has made his last fight, and got whipped! His mate has gone. 'Twas no use for her to stay an try to help him any longer, for she knows he's dead. Now, with the heave and haul of the tide, there is more danger of breaking the line an losing him than if he was alive; but here he comes, an here goes the gaff—a forty-pounder at least!

*S.*   Well done, Mosier! Struck just in time, for the hook has let go.

*Mosier.*   Jist so; I hain't no confidence in them hooks with the barb curling out so that you can not git it into the flesh. The Kinsey point an Sproat bend, or the O'Shaughnessy with the Kinsey point, are the best.

*D.*   Well, my preconceived notions of bass-fishing have all been cast wide. When you first hooked the bass, I thought I could take a seat and be a quiet looker-on at the play; but I have been so excited by alternate hopes, fears, doubts, and surprises, that I want you to pardon me for getting into your way several times. The truth is, it astonishes me to see the fish on *terra firma*. I thought him lost a dozen times; and I can not now fully realize how it is possible to play successfully so large a fish, and one so game, in such boisterous water, with such slender tackle. I am really afraid to try to make a cast, for I expect if I get a strike that I shall either break my rod, or the fish will part my line.

*S.*   Hoot! doctor, don't be too modest; a man who has shot wolves in the Black Forest, and killed salmon in the Dee and Moisie, is not easily demoralized by a striped bass.

*Mosier.*   Yes, doctor, you jist make a cast out into the Rifle Pit, and do it right away, for I see by their whirls that they are hungry.

*S.*   See that your thumb-stalls are well on, and that your line is clear. Now reel up so that your bait is within two feet of the tip of your rod, and when you cast, hold your thumb gently on the reel-line, and as the bait touches the water, press your thumb on the line to check the reel at once, and prevent the reel from over-running.

*D.*   Well, here goes for a second trial.

*S.*   Very fair cast; far enough for bass at this stage of tide.

*D.*   Ye—ye—es, I see it is, but then I shall not be able to save him—I know I can not, for he runs and pulls so like a reindeer that I can not check him. There! my thumb-stall is loose, and I feel that my reel is not tight. He's gone! I knew I couldn't save him.

*S.*   Don't be so excited, doctor; keep cool, and reel in your slack line; he is only studying a new dodge or making a new tack.

*Mosier.*   He breaks water; I seen him; he's a scrounger!

*S.*   There, doctor, you perceive he has hove to for a lunar, and to discover how to tack; there! he is now laying his course for Newport; reel as fast as you can, and, if necessary, run back to prevent him from getting slack line.

*D.*   This last turn and the dash of spray nearly capsized me. Why, he plays as strong as he did when he was first hooked.

*S.*   How long do you suppose you have played him?

*D.*   Nearly an hour, and he seems to grow stronger and stronger.

*S.*   It is not yet fifteen minutes since you hooked him; bear up, keep cool, and keep your line clear on the reel, and be prepared for his fight. They do not appear to be in a mood for sulking this morning; sometimes they settle behind rocks, and butt the hook against them to spring it out.

*Mosier.*   Don't you hold him a leetle to taut?

*D.*   I don't know; but I can not play him easier, for when I give him an inch, he takes a rod!

*S.*   He will soon stop for his final fight. See! he is preparing. Now ease the line a trifle, and trust to the chance of his being well hooked.

*D.*   He's gone, I know he is! Just see the fellow throw himself like Pat McAroon in a street-fight. There, he's off! No, he is not; what's to be done?

*S.*   Reel up gently; he is dead; that, he has fought until he has fainted. Gingerly, doctor; reel with the incoming surf, and slacken with the ebb—there!

*Mosier.*   He is a game one, and will weigh over twenty pounds. They're allays hifalorum in them Rifle Pits! Gentlemen, the breakfast horns has been blowin a good while.

*D.*   I am wilted. These rocks are rough to run about on and play a fish, when every now and then Neptune drenches one with spray. I had long heard that striped bass were game, but all that I ever heard or read did not prepare me for such encounters as I have seen and realized this morning. I am not now surprised that Americans consider this the head of game fishes. The accessories of fishing for it, the scenes where it is taken, together with the *modus operandi* of its capture by artistic means, render the sport the most exciting that I know of under the head of angling. I shall certainly prescribe something to steady my nerves. *Eh bien!* To breakfast is the order; and as we have taken two grand bass, *ne quid nimis*, we will even leave off fishing while they are feeding, which, for the vulgar object of ourselves feeding, is, with a real angler, an unpardonable offense against the aesthetics of sport. But, though belonging to the refined confraternity of anglers, our excuse is that we are rigged with human necessities.

*The scientific angler is master of the situation; he can reach any part of the current, casting into eddies at the base of the precipitous cliffs opposite; he can yield to the rush of the prey; can retire, paying out line, to surer footing, and can follow the fish along the shore; and finally, having subdued his spirit and broken his strength, can lead the prize, gleaming through the transparent water with the sun's rays reflected in rainbow colors from his scales, into some quiet nook where he can gaff him with safety. Such is fly-fishing for striped bass amid the most lovely scenery, gorgeous in its summer dress of green and alternating hill and valley, dotted with pretty farms and smiling grain-fields; and there is but little sport that can surpass it.*

—ROBERT BARNWELL ROOSEVELT,
*Superior Fishing; Or the Striped Bass, Trout, Black Bass,*
*and Blue-Fish of the Northern States, 1884*

# 3

# In Search of the Striped Bass

*T. Coraghessan Boyle*

*Although angling is the traditional and obvious means by which to enjoy the striper, there can be deep pleasure in simply handling such a splendid fish. T. Coraghessan Boyle, a novelist who has enjoyed considerable success in the literary world, reflects in his essay, In Search of the Striped Bass (1992), Boyle reflects on a season spent catching stripers in nets for a hatchery operation on the Hudson River—what he calls ". . . the best job I ever had."*

Ah: But why were we pursuing *Morone saxatilis*, a fish that never did anyone a lick of harm, and why would I have this very photo nailed to the wall just over the photocopier in my office all these many years later?

I had just completed my first year as an M.F.A. and Ph.D. aspirant at the Iowa Writers' Workshop, had acquitted myself well, written a few stories and won a fellowship for the following year. But I was feeling effete and pasty-faced, my spine humped to the contours of my warped and tilting imitation oak desk ($2 at a yard sale in Iowa City), my brain clogged with literature, my feisty backwoods rail-splitting Bunyanesque side shrunk to the size of the flea that infests

This photo shows four rugged Hudson River fishermen in a pose that owes not a little to Huck Finn and Tom Sawyer. It was taken in the spring of 1973 at the Garrison Landing after a seining expedition in search of the mighty and elusive striped bass (*Morone saxatilis*), then in full spawning splendor. I am standing dead smack in the center of this picture. To my right is my boss and head of the expeditionary force, Garrett McCarey, and to his right is Davey McGahee; to my left is John Cutten. (Photo © Rob Jordan, reprinted by permission of Rob Jordan. Originally appeared in *Life.*)

the flea clinging to a deer mouse's whiskers. It was small, that spirit. Moribund. Nearly extinct. So I hied me back to the scenes of my boyhood in search of a summer job that might revivify it.

I started out bartending, as I'd done the year previous on my way to Iowa, and for a few days I poured aquavit and Chartreuse in the late-night glow of neon and grew pastier still—not to mention drunker and more restless. It was then that I discovered that two of my old friends and sinful companions of the past, the aforementioned McCarey and McGahee, were working on the river. The River! The mighty turgid Manhattan-washing pure-stream-and-sewage-fed Hudson, inspiration of Cole and Irving and two of the last and most gracious commercial fishermen then left on its banks, Ace Lent and Charlie White.

Their job? Prowling the river with the tides and netting fat-mouthed stripers gravid with eggs and slick with sperm, in the hope of combining those two elements in a bucket, and then in a lab that would become a hatchery, funded by Con Ed (out of shame and concern for the fish killed on its intake screens at the Indian Point nuclear facility) and overseen by N.Y.U. Their need? For two more grunts to set those nets and haul those ropes. I became an estuarine biologist. Temporarily. And of sorts.

The thing I loved most about the job was its sheer physicality combined with its proximity to nature. There are few excitements to rate with closing off a beach seine, drawing the bag ever tighter as the water churns with the sunstruck snouts, puckered mouths and stabbing dorsals of a grab bag of fish, and then dashing in amongst them to snatch up 30- and 40-pound specimens by the gills . . . if you're a piscaphile, that is. If you're not, better you should purchase a cheesecloth net and engage in fritillary pursuits.

But I loved it. Throve on it. Grew hardened and brown, hands scraped raw from the translucent sandpaper teeth of striper and gill of carp, skin encrusted with scale and slime, waders speckled with milt. And when I—when we—stepped into a bar at night, redolent of the day's endeavors, we were a force to reckon with—and not only on the olfactory level. We were as calm as prayer wheel watchers, we ached in our shoulders and arms in a way that makes pain a pleasure, and when we took up beers in the rough grip of our fishermen's hands, we knew we'd earned them.

This was a job that dispensed with intellectualizing. We were the crew, the seine pullers and carp wrestlers (and they get nigh on to colossal on the Hudson, up in the range of 50 and 60 pounds), and we weren't expected to speak to the finer points of the operation. No, this was the province of the host of pasty-faced, spine-humped, formalin-breathing marine biologists and Ph.D. candidates who crowded round us as we returned from one expedition or another with that bucket of plenty, that liquid gold, those eggs and that milt, those embryos in embryo.

I have held those writhing bass in my arms like a piscine lover, I have milked those vents of their sperm and their eggs, and it was a mighty gratifying—not to mention sensual—experience. I will never forget it. Not as long as I stand humpbacked and whey-faced over my copier, the spirit shrunk in me again, my shoulders yearning for the pull of a good rope, a fat seine and a fish wrapped in its slime like a gift, a hope, a persistent nagging fragment of the great mystery poking its shining snout in my own.

It was the best job I ever had.

*A shapely fish, moreover; active and graceful in its movements; beautiful far above the average of the game-fishes in its silvery mail and brilliant iridescence; quick to seize a suitable lure and to hold it firmly; full of resources in its struggle against capture; full of expedients for escaping the hook or parting the most approved line; endowed with wonderful strength and endurance; quick to take advantage of all the natural obstructions to the angler's skill which exist in its favorite haunts,— the striped bass is a king among the game-fishes.*

—WILLIAM C. HARRIS AND TARLETON H. BEAN,
*The Basses Fresh-Water and Marine, 1905*

# 4

# Angling for Striped Bass

Leonard Hulit

L eonard Hulit was intimately familiar with the inshore fishes of the
Atlantic coast, writing with great authority on how and where to
catch them. But unlike many angling writers of his time, he stressed con-
servation, consideration, and a philosophy that ". . . not all of fishing is to
catch fish." In The Salt Water Angler (1924), a book primarily about surf
fishing, Hulit introduces the striped bass and some of the means by which
it may be taken, followed by a sketch of a dawn encounter with a large
striper.

---

To the striped bass must be given, if to any of our coastal fishes, the
title of gentleman among his tribe. Paeans of praise have been sung
to the lordly salmon of the cascade and mountain stream, and to
*fontinalis* libraries of books have been devoted to illustrate the glories
of his quest and conquest; and it may justly be stated that nothing
has been said of him that cannot find warrant for the effort.

If we claim that trout and salmon fishermen are immaculate in their ideas of proper outfitting, the same must be applied to the bass fishing enthusiast.

It is June, the month of roses and bass, the hour three A.M., when we see our properly equipped angler step from his home and direct his steps toward the beach. The morning stars are yet shining. He is a man of experience and care. His canvas fishing suit and well fitting rubber boots reaching to the thighs witness that fact. A leather rest for his rod butt is around his waist and a well oiled, carefully kept 2-0 or maybe 3-0 reel is on a perfectly balanced greenheart or split bamboo surf rod, agate mounted throughout. That he is a man of experience may be known by the way his eye ranges up and down the beach. The deep water slues do not hold his attention. His mind is on the adjacent flat where the water of the now rising tide comes tumbling over to meet the deep waters in the basin, for well he knows that if a bass is to be taken it is at the point where the troubled waters are washing out the crustacea of the sea.

That he is methodical may be known from the manner in which he prepares. First, six or eight feet of line is stripped from the reel and carefully tested as to strength, as the ends of lines chafe rapidly in surf fishing. Satisfied as to its condition, the four-ply gut leader, with its brass swivel attached, is well secured to the line. Next, the 7-0 O'Shaughnessy hook loop, snelled with four-ply selected gut, is bent on and the point of the hook is tested to determine its condition. It is apparently not to his liking and a small piece of very fine emery cloth is produced from somewhere in his kit and a few smart rubs puts the hook to a needle point.

You will observe that, tied to one eye of the swivel, is a short piece of line with an open loop. If a novice you will ask why. That short piece of line, my friend, is really one of the important parts of the whole outfit. To the loop is fastened the four-ounce casting sinker, which is pyramid in shape and being so shaped holds to the sandy bottom better than any other type yet devised. And as to the importance of the short line you will note that it is tied to the eye of the swivel opposite to the one holding line and leader; this arrangement permits the leader to remain perfectly free of the sinker and the slightest touch on the bait can be felt before the sinker is disturbed.

All being in readiness the angler, before baiting his hook, steps down and makes a short cast, thoroughly wetting down his line, and no matter what bait he may have selected for his trial it is as carefully selected as the other details have been carried out. If bloodworms, two or three are on the hook, with ends hanging free. And now comes a most important part of the program—the cast. The rod is never circled, but the tip is dropped down in front on a line with the eye, then brought back over the right shoulder, then with lightning-like movement the lead is shot out one hundred and fifty, possibly two hundred feet, depositing the baited hook just where the green water is tumbling into the basin.

Years of experience have taught our angler patience and well he knows that this morning may pass as well as many others before the coveted prize is secured, so lighting his pipe he seats himself on his fishing basket and prepares to await events. The tide is propitious, however, and we note how carefully the line is kept just taut, not enough to move the sinker, but just so nicely balanced that the least disturbance of the bait will be telegraphed to the index finger over which the line is drawn.

The first rays of the morning sun are dancing on the waves when our friend springs to his feet. He does not strike, but stands in an attitude of tense expectancy. A quick backward step is taken and the rod, bending like a drawn bow, tells us that the strike has been made. Away out yonder a beautiful creature vaults into the air and dropping back sends a thousand watery diamonds high into the air. The singing reel assures us that the steel barb is locked in the fish's mouth and it is now a battle of wits between man and quarry. But the man is ripe with experience. At the first rush the click has been set on his reel so that in the event of a misstep there will be no overrunning of the line on the spool of the reel. At first the startled fish battles in the shallow water. Away he goes, two, perhaps three hundred feet, at the first rush, his beautiful contour showing plainly as he cuts through the waves. We note that his first rush is to the north; now he doubles and comes back with arrowlike swiftness and we hold our breath as the line slackens, but our friend attends to that; he steps back quickly and, reeling in fast, soon brings the line taut. Again the tactics are gone through, not so far this time, however. Finding no relief from his bondage the fish now seeks deep water and sulks, but the gentle springing of the rod tells us he is being prodded into action. We notice now he is swimming in circles, a sure sign of waning powers in a fish. The end is not yet, however; again, and yet again, he is worked to the beach and as often goes to deep water. Once more the sulking tactics are brought into play, only to be broken up by the master hand at the rod, until the fast tiring fish is worked into the trough of the sea near the beach. Now the whole beautiful struggling creature is in full view, swimming parallel with the beach, his powerful tail beating the water and every fin set abrace against the action of the threadlike line from which he cannot get release.

The fire in his eye is plainly visible as each succeeding wave lifts him gradually toward the sands. Steady now, my man; your fateful moment is at hand. You have a prize fit for ransom within your grasp. A moment's carelessness now and all may be lost to you. But he knows a thing or two of the game; the line will not be slackened. As the waves throw the fish upon the sands he steps slowly backward keeping the line taut until the prize is won. And such a prize—the striped monarch of the Atlantic coast, about forty pounds of him—every inch is beauty and every ounce meant battle.

*No angling can surpass*
*The taking of the basse.*

—JOHN J. BROWN, *The American Angler's Guide,* 1876

# 5

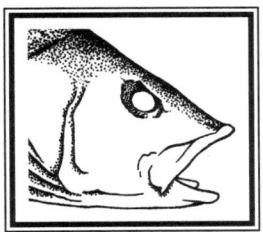

# Forecasting Stripers

*Phil Schwind*

*C* | *ape Cod is a low-lying world of sand and water; elbowing far into the Atlantic, its wave-battered outer beaches, clear bay waters, and powerful riptides offer superior striped bass angling. In* Cape Cod Fisherman *(1974), charter boat captain Phil Schwind tells of a life spent pursuing the Cape's stripers. This excerpt concerns forecasting the date of the springtime appearance of striped bass—a much discussed subject on Cape Cod and the rest of the New England coast where stripers are sorely missed after a winter's absence.*

---

On the way home nights I used to stop in at the Players' Pharmacy for a cup of hot coffee. Lennie Dubin, one of the brother-proprietors, kidded me every night. "You the great striper fisherman! No stripers tonight?"

I'd say, "Not yet, Lennie, it's still too early." Then came the day when the mackerel gulls showed up, dipping and wheeling as they do only when they come back in the spring, greeting me once again with the "Fe-e-esh, fe-e-esh, fe-e-esh" call that gives them the name of "liar birds." That night I said in answer to Lennie's kidding, "Two weeks from today, Lennie. Today's Wednesday. A week from next Wednesday when I come ashore I'll show you some stripers."

He laughed and kidded and had a wonderful time. For my part, I had no idea the old-timers were so right. Frank, I think it was, had told me that stripers show up two weeks to the day after the common terns. And they did.

I had dragged nine bushels of scallops and was working on my last one. Now, I've said *Nonny* was a little boat, and all the gear, plus forty fathoms of three-quarter-inch manila rope jumbled on the deck, plus nine full bags of sea scallops in the shell, didn't leave an awful lot of clear deck room. I had just hauled back on what was scheduled to be my last tow of the day when I looked up—and all the birds in the world were going crazy a mile or so offshore: mackerel gulls, herring gulls, gannets, and even an occasional loon.

I dumped the drag, rocks and all, with the scallops on the culling board, slipped off the belts from the winch, and headed for my kind of fishing. I flopped down the outriggers and secured them. For all my care in coiling down the handlines, they had somehow got tangled, so I was nearly into breaking stripers before I could get the first lure over. I cut the motor to trolling speed and jumped for the other handline, which was in an even worse mess than the first one. Before I could get that lure free I had a fish on the first line. Not a big fish, only fourteen to sixteen pounds, but the first striper nevertheless. I hauled him in, welcomed him aboard with a clout between the eyes, chucked over the rig and went for that snarled handline. I needn't have hurried. I picked up one more fish the same size and that was all. They sounded. I had no idea how long they had been up and feeding, but, as always, they can disappear in an awful hurry.

I went round and round, trolling two lines. Finally I went to cutting my scallops, not shucking the guts overboard as usual, but throwing them onto the culling board. When I had finished my ten gallons I kept on trolling and watching; then I began to strike my scallop gear. I'd had enough sea-scalloping for that year. First the boom came down, and all the blocks supporting it, then the mast and guys, then the winch, and I even unbolted the culling board. I could tell *Nonny* was feeling fancier and freer all the time.

Finally I gave up for the day, dumped the culling board and went ashore. I began to grin—two weeks to the day! Would I ever rub it into Lennie tonight! I carried home all the gear that poor Model A could stagger under, leaving the rest on the shore for the next day. I stopped in for my usual cup of coffee—and don't you know that Lennie never said a word about what day it was, and when would the stripers be here?

Not one minute longer could I stand it. "Lennie," I asked innocently, "what day is it anyway?"

"The fourteenth, but what day of the week?"

"Wednesday ... Oh, yeah, Wednesday. This is the day the stripers were due. Well, where are they?"

I said as casually as I could, though I was squirming with glee, "Oh, they're in the back of my car, under all the gear."

"Oh, sure," he said, "oh, yeah. 'Two weeks from the day the mackerel gulls get here,' he said, now he wants to sucker me into going out to look in the back of his car."

"Suit yourself. I don't care if you want to look at them." (I'd never have forgiven him if he hadn't.) "Why else do you suppose I've got the mast and boom lashed alongside the car?"

That convinced him. He went out to look and admire. He told it all over town for the next summer that I could tell when the fish were going to get here two weeks before they actually did.

# 6

# Surf Fishing

Van Campen Heilner and Frank Stick

*J* ust after the turn of the century, the south Jersey shore was a much
wilder place than it is today, rich in fish and home to pioneering
surfcasters who sometimes spent days camping on the dunes. Two prodi-
gies of New Jersey beach fishing, Van Campen Heilner and Frank Stick,
co-authored The Call of the Surf (1924), the first book solely about surf-
casting. With youthful exuberance, they chronicled their adventures in
landing a suite of fishes, from black drum and channel bass, to bonito
and large sharks. In this account, Stick describes a morning on the beach
spent with an old timer and a contrary striper.

There had been a great run of striped bass along the Jersey shore.
Tide would be full about eight, and as the best of the fishing ordinar-
ily came the last couple of hours of flood, Art and I landed upon the
beach a half hour or so before sun-up with our outfits and a goodly
mess of clams all nicely cleaned.

Other fishermen were on the beach before us this morning as the
glimmering campfires above and below us attested. One of two shad-

owy figures were in evidence, also, as we waded into the surf and made our casts.

After a bit a glint of rosy light showed low in the sky, which spread and brightened perceptibly with each minute that passed, and almost before we were conscious of the fact it was daylight. A blue-gray morning, with white spume drifting in from the sea, and the low breakers sending their froth about our ankles. I knew the lay of the beach, and I had chosen to fish a deep hole while the tide was making, for I have a theory that bass are in the habit of feeding in deep water during low and half tide, and moving to the flats for clams and mussels at flood.

A hundred yards north of us I saw our nearest neighbour working with a fish, and presently he stooped and carried up the beach a small specimen of seven or eight pounds. I had raised my head to call my companion's attention to this interesting development when I saw his line straighten with a jerk, and at the same instant his rod flashed backward. This fish made a short run of fifty feet or so, then swam parallel with the beach until Art had worked him into a roller which carried him gently high and dry up on the sand. This was another small fellow. Not large enough to put any strain on the tackle or the fisherman, but an excellent weight for the pan.

I changed my position after this capture, and cast into a swirl of green, frothy water, which marked a flat. For an hour or more I held the rod, only bringing in my cast at intervals to renew the bait, for clams, besides being the natural food for stripers, are much relished by crabs which were plentiful at this point.

Presently I was joined by a grizzled old fellow who had put in the night a-fishing without result. A garrulous old chap of long acquaintances, and he proceeded to enlighten me upon the habits of salt-water fish in general, and in particular upon the peculiar traits of stripers. He assured me that there was not the slightest use in fishing at this time of tide. To which I replied by baiting afresh, and making a short cast into the ruffled water. Seeing that I was not one to profit by his advice, he proceeded to recount for my edification a recent experience. It seemed that a day or two previous he had hooked what he claimed to be a gold medal fish, which means one of twenty-five pounds or better, and had worked him into the undertow after an exciting combat.

"The waves were running high," he said, gesticulating with both hands in order to show me the exact height and shape of the waves in question, "and three times they brought that there fish in, and laid him at my feet, and three times they took and snatched him from my hands. At last I sez to myself, do or die. Do or die, sez I, and the next time the fish was fetched in, I up and grabbed the line with my two hands and laid back on her—"

I do not know, I probably never will know, whether that line held or whether it gave way under the strain put upon it, for at this point in his narrative I felt a lift, and as the hook was set, my line shot out from the reel.

For an instant my companion stood, with bulging eyes and with widespread arms delineating the last scene in his recent encounter. Then: "By gosh, you've hooked into one!" he shouted, and leaped into the air with the agility of a boy.

"Now take it easy, an' don't get excited," he counselled, snatching his hat from his head and slapping it against his thigh. "Give him line, an' don't snub him or you'll lose him sure pop," he warned me as the fish bore seaward. And all through the battle the old fellow persisted in shouting his advice and his admonitions to be calm, to none of which did I pay the slightest heed, for my mind was fully occupied with the work before me.

One long run the striper made, then worked southward toward a long jetty which reached into the ocean, and only by vigorous pumping did I succeed in turning him in the opposite direction, and keep him from fouling. Another rush, but shorter this time, then foot by foot I worked him toward shore. At last he came close in to the breakers, where the beach shelved off abruptly, and from this point I did not seem able to budge him. Back and forth, to and fro, he swam, until at last, as I felt his struggles lessening, I put a bit more strain on the line. He came to me then, on a curling wave, and slipping my fingers beneath his gills I dragged him up the beach.

There was a ringing yell in my ear, and a heavy hand swatted me betwixt the shoulders.

"I knew you could do it," a voice shouted. "I knew if you followed my advice, an' kept calm like I told you, you'd land him, and he's a medal fish, sure as you're born."

This is surf fishing, as it is practised at a thousand points along our shores, though not always with success to equal the examples I have given. And yet, not infrequently the results will be far more satisfying.

A man may spend a day on the beach and come home at evening

with an empty basket, and yet count the day not wasted. Many things there are to be caught besides fish: the sunlight, the salty breeze that sweeps the dunes, healthful exercise. And also, there is a certain satisfaction of the soul which comes to most of us when old ocean rolls before our eyes. There is a vastness about it, and yet restfulness. Power and strength are expressed in every breaker, and yet the sonorous beat of them lulls us to sleep. The omnipotence of it all assures us of our own insignificance and unimportance in the scheme of nature, but at the same time it satisfies us of the futility of worry and complaint over the small irritations of life. Personally, I believe that after a day or a week beside the blue water I come home a better man, and if the results are not permanent, it is no fault of my tutor. At least I am sure that I return happier, and more contented, and younger in spirit and in body.

*I had been fishing for some hours without success; and as the now large waves rolled in, my eye followed them in, commenting on their remarkable clearness and transparency. I made a new cast, and sat down, when on my left, heading for the bait which I had just thrown out, was a beautiful bass, his stripes and silver side plainly visible, his brilliant eyes staring at me, precisely as mine were fixed on him. The wave rolled him up until he was in bold relief against its green depths; and had he been artificially held there, the picture could not have been more perfect nor animated. His impetus and intention both carried him as far as the bait; and he took it into his mouth, but only held it for an instant. His terror was too vivid to admit of forgetfulness; and I in vain reeled in, and threw again and again.*

—A. FOSTER HIGGINS,
"Striped Bass Fishing," in *Angling,* 1896

# 7

# Night Moves

*Russell Chatham*

*T* | *he heart of many a coastal city arcs around its harbor, yet there is*
*wonderful irony in the solitude that sometimes can be experienced at*
*night on the urban waterfront. But finding striper fishing spots in the inter-*
*stitial spaces of a developed metropolitan shoreline often requires much*
*prospecting and a little trespassing—with occasional surprise encounters—*
*so that prime locations must be fished with discretion. In Night Moves*
*(1988), Russell Chatham illustrates the lengths to which guerilla striper*
*fishermen will go to protect the privacy of a favored locale in San Francisco*
*Bay.*

---

There is a shallow arm of San Francisco Bay, which, during the
twenty years I lived in the area, was within ten minutes of my house.
The place was so spartan, so unappealing in the light of day, so geo-
metric and outwardly perverse, that fishermen overlooked it entirely.
If you had pointed it out to a trout fisherman he would have wanted
to throw up.

As a striped bass fisherman I saw something else. Looking for
special purposes beyond the inexcusable damage done by industrial

and civic disregard, I found a place to catch bass as large as thirty pounds or more, by fly casting from shore.

At that time, in the early- to mid-sixties, there were plenty of stripers, and many different places to fish for them. I literally did so every day from about 1955 until 1970, when I moved to Montana. During that time the fishing did nothing but improve. This secret hole was a pleasure largely because going there was not expeditionary. It was a little like having a spring creek winding through your yard.

A look at the tide and current tables gave a starting point: low tide. From there I determined the part of the flood I wanted to catch and at what time. There was room for two fishermen. But this was one of those fragile, precise situations which defined the thinness of the line between failure and success. Success here meant fishing a very exact edge of the current at a certain hour, and from one angle in particular. At the time it seemed gravely important that absolutely none of this data fall into the wrong hands, i.e., the hands of anyone who ever even vaguely considered owning a fishing rod.

Now, urban life has never been known to dull the primordial urge to fish. I know one New Yorker, the author Nick Lyons, whose excellent and popular prose more often than not deals with the conflict between his need to be a city dweller in order to make a living and his strong desire to spend time alone along quiet waters. Others, like Guy DeBlasio, armed with a large billy club and matching cajones, take their light tackle of an evening and head straight for the Harlem River.

In San Francisco, which is to New York what fresh *linguine alla Vongole* is to rat poison, I frequently saw people loading tackle into their cars in the early morning, especially in the quiet neighborhoods. Most stayed close to town, fishing from piers, beaches or rocks. Others went to the waterfront to take a boat out on the bay or ocean. Still others, depending upon the season, went out of town an hour or two after steelhead, salmon, trout, shad or black bass.

Some of the men were construction workers, some had desk jobs at City Hall, some were Montgomery Street brokers, bankers or executives. Others worked in department stores, restaurants, banks or shops. A number were elderly or unemployed and lived in buildings now toppled in the name of urban renewal. It didn't matter. A phone call to someone with a screening secretary was put through twice as quickly if it was about fishing than if it had to do with actual business.

There was something to be said about finding one's sport close to home (excepting, of course, an illicit session of the horizontal mambo). Brochure esthetics and the often outrageous outdoor magazine promises invariably failed to compare with the rich skein of knowledge which results from simply paying attention at home.

I remember one evening some years back when a friend and I had all the luck in the world at our secret hole. We had decided a new ruse was needed *vis-à-vis* concealing the car, and ended up leaving it about 600 yards away at a commuter bus stop. It was after dark as we slipped over a low embankment to start the fifteen minute walk through weedy, uneven marshland and acres of debris. My friend had a pair of black waders, the kind so popular in New Zealand, a black parka and a black wool stocking cap. When I kidded him about face paint he replied that someday I was going to give the whole thing away by wearing loud clothing like my snot green sweater.

The cool evening air was unusually still that night. It was not, however, in any sense quiet, and we had to converse in voices loud enough to be heard over the heavy drone of nearby traffic. Around us the landscape was complicated, inorganic, industrial; piers, bridges and docks gave way to frontage roads, restaurants, service stations, office buildings, apartments, condominiums, and a galaxy of night lights.

When we reached our destination—a complex of pilings just a few yards out from the muddy bank—the tide was slack low. We sat down on a large pipe, in all likelihood a sewer, to wait for the flood to begin. Nearby was a sharply curved off-ramp which, to judge by the constant squeal of tires, most cars took a little too fast. As we sat talking, there was a sharp screech of rubber against asphalt and a tremendous crash. Within minutes the highway patrol was there, red and yellow beacons flashing, reflecting off the water and freeway abutments like a sixties Fillmore Auditorium light show. Soon a tow truck was tacking into position near the twisted metal and broken light filaments, as police radios crackled loudly in the night.

We both saw the figure moving toward us along the pedestrian walkway. It seemed preposterous to make a run for it like fugitives, and there was really no place to hide. There was simply nothing to do but stand up and start walking casually as if it were the most normal thing in the world to be strolling around under the freeway in the middle of the night in waders and carrying fly rods.

"I think we're safe," I whispered. We tried to look as inconspicuous as possible. "This guy looks drunk as a skunk to me."

And drunk he was as he passed by without even acknowledging our presence. But his reaction was merely delayed.

"Hey! You guys!"

We stopped and turned slowly.

"Been fishin'?"

"Uh . . . sort of."

"Get any?"

"No."

"Yer doin' it wrong. It's the wrong night. C'mere. Yer gonna think I'm blowin' smoke at ya. You think I'm blowin' smoke at ya I know, but I've seen 'em *this big*!" He jabbered, and held out his hands to indicate a large fish.

"Now, I'm drunk. I been drinkin'. Okay. But I swear I'm not makin' this up. I've seen 'em jumpin' by those pilings."

My friend and I looked at each other, both thinking the same thing: was this how the fickle finger of fate was going to deliver our secret into the hands of the public domain, through this blabbermouth telling everyone who would listen about big fish jumping all over the place just minutes from the tavern?

"I know, I know," he went on holding his hands and arms outstretched in a gesture that made him look like he was supporting a leaning panel of plywood with his fingertips and forehead. "You guys think I'm blowin' smoke at ya. Believe me now, second full moon of the summer. Warm night. Be here. See, the mosquitoes fly down by the water to keep cool, and the big fish are right there waitin' for 'em."

We laughed and thanked him for the terrific advice, and enthusiastically convinced him we didn't think he was blowing smoke at us. Seeing we took him seriously seemed to give him great pleasure. We promised to return at the time of the second full moon (whatever or whenever that was), but only if he agreed not to spread the news further. He went on his way, humming.

Back at our station the tide began to move. In the wake of some pilings, distant lights glinted off tiny folds in the current. As the water gained momentum, bits of food would be dislodged and small forage fish disoriented. When the tide reached a particular pitch, we hoped to see the first feeders explode out on the dark edge of the channel as the predators sensed it was time.

A patch of reasonably intact marsh lay near where we fished, its light green grasses lush and dense. A wooden structure built at the turn of the century still stood at its edge. Something old did remain. The years had laminated their influence upon the countryside, but certain places were covered more slowly than others; some not at all. This phenomenon is a bit like fattening a picture over the under-painting; paint and repaint, yet in the end certain areas are finalized by being left alone. You lose the habit of rifling through the pages of time, perhaps because mental health rests in some large measure on coming to terms with the present. So, oddly enough, it took me a while to realize that the "secret riffle" as Myron Gregory used to call it, was mere yards from where my mother and her family lived in the early decades of the twentieth century.

They lived on a houseboat, one of many which then lined the little slough. My grandfather, Gottardo Piazzoni, a painter, did sketches of the arks, the bay, and the surrounding hills. Rich paintings, soundly constructed and sensitive in every detail, which recorded moods of solitude, peace and warmth. These beautiful works gave no notice whatsoever of the coming of condominiums, freeways or the Army Corps of Engineers.

But come they did. The two-lane country road and wooden drawbridge were replaced by ten lanes and soaring overpasses. The arks, simply yet elegantly built by ship chandlers, were easily smashed into flotsam by the massive blades of efficient D9's. Dissatisfied with intimate, serpentine creeks and sloughs, the Corps dredged and straightened every mystery out of them, leaving behind bare, evenly beveled shores unfriendly to herons and mallards. The landscape was given a giant manicure, polished off with apartment complexes, shopping malls and a seemingly endless number of fast-food establishments.

Oddly enough, at the time there was still something intact about the water itself. After a century of increasing pollution, public indignation had finally begun to turn the situation around. People were not only calling for an end to indiscriminate dredging and filling of the bay's shoreline, but were also demanding that neither industries nor cities be allowed to release untreated waste into the water. To everyone's astonishment, about a decade and a half ago the bay was cleaner than it had been for sixty years. Biologists discovered forms of marine life on San Francisco's waterfront not seen there in more than half a century.

At the same time, the population of striped bass was far larger than it had ever been. Runs recorded by the durable Leon Adams in his long-standing classic, *Striped Bass Fishing in California and Oregon*, began to reappear after having been nonexistent since Truman was president.

In 1965 I caught nearly a thousand bass by fly fishing, killing only about a dozen of those. Then in 1966 I was lucky enough to land a thirty-six-pound striper which became a new world record on the fly. The previous record—a twenty-nine-pound striper caught by the late Joe Brooks—had stood for eighteen years. All reasonable leads panned out: there didn't seem to be any place where you couldn't catch bass.

Before long, a small fish hopped erratically from the water, hotly pursued by a striped bass. My friend landed a cast in the right place and had a take immediately. His fish pulled to one side, giving me room to cast to others which had begun to feed. My streamer was soon hit and we were both connected to struggling fish. We landed them and made a bed of rushes to hide them in the dark.

It was a good night and the bass fed wantonly, visibly reckless as they slashed into an endless buffet of bright silver smelt. Within two hours, four more stripers were hidden in the reeds. The smallest weighed at least fifteen pounds, the largest about twenty-five, our lawful limit. In any quarter it was a very impressive catch, made all the more so by the difficult and arcane craft of fly casting, and taken under the noses of ten thousand speeding cars while we fished in a kind of solitude as complete in its own way as that of the Canadian Rockies.

We decided one of us should get the car so we wouldn't have to carry everything so far. It was late enough that few people were around. Just as everything was put away, headlights beamed over us, then a spotlight. The patrol car pulled right up behind us.

"Be cool, it's nothing," my friend advised.

Two officers got out, and the first said, "Sheriff's Department. Everything okay?"

"Oh . . . well . . . uh, we just thought we'd stop for a little air, walk around, look at the water, you know, get outside."

"Here? You boys have some identification?"

We have him our driver's licenses and the second officer took them to the car.

"Kind of an odd place to be getting air, isn't it?" the first deputy said, looking at us, then at the surrounding area.

"Officer," my friend began earnestly, "maybe we'll get into less trouble if we just level with you. We were shooting a little pool at that bar about five blocks from here when we decided to step out and smoke a little number, you know? Didn't think we'd be bothered down here."

"You have any more stuff in the car?"

"One joint was it."

The second officer came back with our licenses. "These are okay."

"You guys get out of here now, and don't be hanging around down here anymore."

After they'd returned to their car I said, "Good Lord, why did you tell him that!"

"Look," my friend explained, "a lot of cops like to fish. They're like firemen. They all fish and hunt. Suppose those two deputies happened to be fishermen? If they found out about this spot they'd go crazy. They could even time their rounds so they could get in a few casts right during the best part of the tide. That would be it. You know how touchy this place is. I had to tell them something they'd believe, something to completely satisfy their curiosity."

"What if they arrested us for drugs?"

"They didn't, did they? And we don't have any, either. If they had wanted to make an issue out of it we would have had to tell the truth. But they didn't."

*A million twinkling stars in a blue-back canopy create an awe-inspiring setting, and one of the most striking sights I have ever seen was a bass which hit a surface plug and leaped clear of the water perfectly silhouetted against a full autumn moon just rising above the horizon.*

—Kib Bramhall, "The World of the Night Surf,"
in *Salt Water Sportsman*, November 1962

# 8

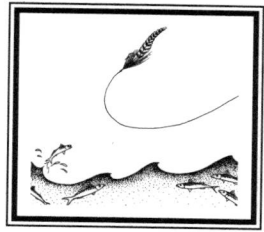

# The Hard Business of Surfcasting

## Frank Woolner

A great deal has been published about how to catch striped bass in the surf, much of the best advice written by Frank Woolner. In The Hard Business of Surf-Casting (1969), Woolner again offers a short course in the mechanics and strategies of surfcasting, but he also delves deeper, introducing the novice to both the spiritual pleasures and harsh realities of the sport. It is a seduction, albeit with warnings, by a hard-boiled romantic.

---

Since about 2 A.M. I had been scuffing along Thoreau's Great Beach on Cape Cod, casting surface plugs and rigged eels out into a heaving, sibilant darkness where breaking waves were ghosts and the horizon was a curious demarcation line of black on black. Then the diamonds disappeared.

Up to this point, each step had unearthed showers of blue-green luminescence in the sand and wash. Billions of microscopic diatoms (*Noctiluca*) were emitting sparks—the "fire in the water" that is so roundly cursed by summer surfmen, because striped bass usually ignore lures bathed in its cold flame. Now strengthening light had dissipated the brilliance of this plankton swarm.

Dawn is a subtle thing in the Northeast: It never arrives with a burst of pyrotechnics, but rather with a gradual paling, so that the horizon swims up like a photoprint in stale developer. Gradually there arc highlights on the ground swells, and one may see an arctic tern curving across the faintly visible world of sand and sea.

I was weary. My waders seemed unbelievably clumsy and a dull ache pierced my shoulder blades. But the tide was right and I was committed. It would be stupid to hit the sack now. Dawn and dusk are the magic periods, especially with a great tide flooding. Muttering about a scarcity of bass, I battled drowsiness. That's another thing about surfmen: We all talk to ourselves. Make the most of it.

Retrieving, I felt the double knot slide under a line-grooved left thumb. Two turns and there'd be just enough overhand for another cast. Mechanically I swiveled, laid the big rod back and brought it forward in an accelerated sweep. Line soughed off the wide-spooled squidding reel, a long trajectory of sound, diminishing until I knew that the lure was touching down. Then I reached over with my left hand and threw the clutch into gear.

Whether it was the strengthening light that dulled the "fire," or just a combination of dawn and flood I do not know, but there was a gout of white spray where my plug had been, together with the familiar, yet always surprising shock of a striper's headlong attack. I was whole again.

Not only whole, but leaning back while my rod tip pounded. Line departed in stuttering zips. The drag was set just tight enough to be punishing, but not screwed to a breaking point. Tight drags lose more game fish than any other single factor. Grimly, I twisted my head to see whether other anglers had witnessed this triumph. Three beach buggies were silhouetted against a slivering curve of beach, but no human stirred. They were all asleep.

Gradually, the bulldogging bass yielded. He thrashed out beyond the third wave—thirty yards away—giving me one glimpse of a shining body and a broom-sized tail. The rolling combers were his ally—and mine, if I could make proper use of them. In close, after each wave exploded on the beach and went surging back to sea, my bass exploited the tremendous power of undertow, so I'd have to grant line. But caught in the next advancing swell, he'd be just as irresistibly borne along, and it would be my time to apply pressure.

Finally, on the crest of a towering swell, the fish was finished. I back-pedaled, maintaining a tight line. Weary, at last, he came flouncing ashore and I ran down to grab the leader, to belt him with a hardwood priest.

Forty pounds of striped bass, silver and lavender and smelling of thyme. Forty pounds of magnificent game fish, glistening in the light of a New England dawn.

It has become customary, in writing about surf-casting to warn the reader that he had best forget the whole thing. Having said this, the writer proceeds at greater or lesser length to extol the delights of a rough-and-tough angling method that offers immense esthetic and, at times, material reward in the shape of great fish. There are two reasons for the admonition. First, of course, it commands attention: Anything advised against must be strangely, if esoterically, delicious. Second, there is more than a bit of truth in the cliché.

As a surf-caster, I have spent a great many years on a variety of beaches, from the cold wash of Maine down through Cape Cod to Hatteras and beyond. I have belted lures at roosterfish on the west coast of Costa Rica and I have worked up the Pacific seaboard to San Francisco. Species change with the latitudes, and each of the great ones requires some variation in lure presentation and tactics, but there is no such sea-change in the surf-caster or the things that make him tick. He is a specialist, quite as thorough a craftsman as the citizen who has learned to drop a lightly cocked bivisible some few yards above a brown trout.

In America, the high surf—and I plead guilty to inventing this term some two decades back to distinguish between ordinary shore fishing conditions and the furious breakers of an outer beach—means striped bass and channel bass. S. Kip Farrington will hate me for excluding South America's great roosterfish (I would agree with him were more of us able to angle for *pez gallo*).

Other formidable gamesters are hooked in the suds: bluefish and weakies, corvina, pompano, and a host of sharks. They're all fine when the time is right, but anglers still associate the great striper of the Northeast and of San Francisco, together with the broad-shouldered channel bass of Virginia's Barrier Islands and North Carolina's Outer Banks, with surf-casting at its furious best.

The striper remains my choice, possibly because I am steeped in New England brine. What makes this fish unique? Other fish-shaped fish can run faster, pull harder, and jump higher. But none is quite so unpredictable—and there is the challenge. When you catch a trophy bass in the 40- to 60-pound bracket, you have achieved something.

Stripers rarely leap after the manner of an Atlantic salmon or tarpon, but they do so occasionally. More typical is the powerful, wallowing surface cartwheel, during which the fish makes much use of its huge, square tail to slap the water. The striped bass is a pugnacious, active gladiator, catholic in its tastes. Therefore, anglers who employ natural bait suffer no handicap. Indeed, there are occasions when the bottom-bouncer outfishes the purist who uses nothing but metal or a treble-hooked plug.

I hope certain chambers of commerce will forgive me if I puncture a few daydreams. Major striper-range extends from the Outer Banks of North Carolina northward into the Maritime Provinces, and, on the Pacific Coast, from San Francisco into the clean rips of Coos Bay, Oregon. In other places, there are landlocked bass, most notably in South Carolina's Santee-Cooper impoundments, and there are stripers in the inland fresh waters of the Gulf of Mexico. If you are seeking trophies, however, range is drastically reduced.

Curiously—because commercial fishermen continue to prove they are there—Chesapeake Bay, the world's foremost striper nursery, rarely produces record-crowding bass for rod-and-line anglers. Similarly, monsters are present on the Outer Banks from early December through February, where they are harvested by haul seiners, yet seldom by sportsmen.

The best fishing begins in New Jersey and extends northward through Long Island and the coasts of Rhode Island and Massachusetts. Connecticut somehow is bypassed by most of the heavyweights during their annual migrations, and Maine is best known for an abundance of schoolies.

On the Pacific seaboard (where the species was introduced during the late nineteenth century), there are two locations of importance to high-surf enthusiasts. One is the Ocean Beach area immediately adjacent to San Francisco's Golden Gate, and the other is Coos Bay. Perhaps the latter is a sleeper, if only because Oregon anglers are prone to place the native king and silver salmon above the imported striper as game.

Zero in, and you will find that all records indicate Massachusetts and Rhode Island to be the principal states for surfers who hunt striped bass. There, more trophy bass are brought to account each year than in all other areas combined. I have enjoyed great sport with

*Roccus* in the Chesapeake, in San Francisco, and at Montauk, but for sheer numbers of heavyweights give me that rugged Yankee coast, bounded by Rhode Island's Charleston Inlet to the south, and Cape Cod to the north.

Moreover, during a New England season, which begins in May and continues through October, this mercurial slugger is taken at all hours of the day and night, a characteristic that guarantees red-eyed, unshaven regulars who live for the next tide and who never admit defeat. Ridiculous people! I am one of them.

In self-defense, if for no other reason, there is a thing about surf-casting that is unique. It is difficult to put into words, because there is no single facet to grasp and to declare typical. I am tempted to say that surf-casting, compared to inland angling, is the difference between elemental fury and tranquility. Wind, fog, crashing combers, and surging currents are the rule on a sea beach. An angler is a combatant, not a seeker of Izaak Walton's gentle relaxation.

Every surfman lives for a "blitz" of bass, and often these frenzied feeding periods coincide with weather guaranteed to keep normal, thoughtful people at home. No wind ever blows too hard for a striper, and no surf dismays the fish. Once, years ago, I caught a bass during that short, glowering period of calm which is called the eye of a hurricane. Again, on Nauset Beach, midway on Cape Cod, I hooked a striper as lightning split a thunderous night sky. In the weird glare of the forking bolt I saw the bass boil up to take a plug and cartwheel wildly. Normally, I'm a first-class coward, but on that night I was fishing with Arnold Laine of Templeton, Massachusetts, a great commercial rod and liner. He wouldn't quit and so, being a stubborn man, neither would I. Throughout that vicious electrical storm, bass walloped our plugs.

Every surfman flirts with disaster—and counts it part of the adventure. Annually, men are washed off wave-battered rock jetties and tumbled in the smothering combers. It is a wet, cold, and thoroughly wonderful business! Still, there are nights when the ocean breathes evenly, when the swells come dreamily ashore, when dim starlight is reflected from a wet silk surface.

Perhaps much of the allure lies in the fact that surfmen probe a last frontier. The roaring ocean remains unconquered, and her fish are no pale descendants of hatchery spawn. Here, the unbelievable is quite possible. I have been startled by a great whale with halitosis (they always have halitosis) bursting out of the inshore swells like something from the prehistoric past. No sea monster is beyond belief in that pale hour of dawn when the ocean pulses and sighs.

Nor is it all nighttime and a sense of things that might be seen, but are not. Beachcombers sometimes observe a sight that is reserved for few men. When the brilliant white light of midmorning lances through advancing combers, one may occasionally see a striped bass suspended in the heart of an emerald wave. No transfixed, split-second image so thoroughly conveys the striper's power as this airy, swift, yet unhurried passage through a comber racing forward, cresting, and aiming its pile-driving power at an unyielding beach.

Nowadays spinning tackle is the preference of the majority. I like coffee grinders, and yet I continue to go back to the old high surf squidding outfit when the fish are big. I think it takes more skill to employ orthodox tackle—although "orthodox" may soon mean another thing if spinning continues to conquer the multitudes.

Whatever the gear, a surfman must be a craftsman, able to cast a lure to extreme range, which means approximately a hundred yards. He must do this instinctively, for there is no time or opportunity to lay the line with mathematical precision during a nighttime retrieve. A man's left thumb becomes educated; it sweeps back and forth like a metronome, geared to the rate of retrieve. Any lump on the orthodox spool will mean a backlash on the next cast.

Spin-casters are not plagued by this difficulty, but they have to live with other handicaps. For one thing, the fixed-spool addict is hard put to throw heavy lures to the distances often required in high surf. Once tied into a fish, there is less control and, because of the light monofilament line used with this rig, a greater degree of peril.

Selection of proper lures is important. There are, for example, about nine basic plug designs, together with many variations, engineered to swim, pop, or skip on the surface, to swim or dart at mid-depths, and to dredge the bottom. Metal squids, forerunners of all modern high-surf tempters, are much used. Natural rigged eels, with or without casting weights attached to their heads, and patent, soft plastic eels are hot items on bass.

Now we deal with tides and currents, with moon phases and "fire in the water." It is necessary to recognize bait and to divine its action as a clue to the proximity of game fish. We must be bird-watchers, too, for the gulls and terns of any seaboard are a surfman's light cavalry. A single striper's slashing attack on bait fish in choppy waters may not be registered by human eyes, but a herring gull or tern, sitting on the beach with its fellows—all facing into the wind like weather vanes—will immediately lift off and speed to the scene. A wheeling, diving gaggle of birds usually means game fish beneath, pushing bait to the surface.

Generally, game fish such as the striped bass prefer to feed in "live water." A general rule of thumb, therefore, holds that fishing will be best "two hours before and two hours after the top of the tide." This is generalization at its best, because rips, inlets, and estuaries change the situation. Moreover, the bass is unpredictable enough to vary his feeding pattern occasionally.

But "live water" is a good phrase, because it means moving water. When water moves, bait is swept along with it—and big fish eat little fish, that's one of the laws of creation. So you're there at the right time, supposedly in the right place, armed with the correct tackle. Add a new dimension: In salt water you'd best be an opportunist, ready to take immediate advantage of anything strange or unusual. The sudden swoop of birds, the twinkling surface flurry of bait, a slick, or even a curious smell.

Any expert surfman can smell striped bass, bluefish, or red drum. Beginners always doubt this, but it is so. The striper exudes a fresh, cloying scent that has been likened to cut melon or thyme. I opt for the latter, believing that cut melon more accurately describes the scent of bluefish. Channel bass throw off a more acrid scent, something almost chemical—and how any of them do this is unresolved. Probably the scent is an excrescence; I don't think anyone knows, but the various aromas are far from imagination. Once isolated they are weapons in the expertise of the surf-caster.

Now I chance incurring the wrath of sportsmen who rely on natural bait alone. I can sympathize with them, for they have much to argue about. The great fishes of our sea rim will take a wide variety of fresh baits, ranging from sea worms and through squid, crabs, mackerel, herring, and sand launces to ordinary clam flesh. There are many natural tempters, and I leave them to the specialists, who will probably rack up a world's-record catch before I tangle with another bona fide trophy. But to me, and evidently to a growing number of marine anglers, there is nothing so satisfactory as a great game fish on an artificial lure. There is something peculiarly gratifying in fooling a sought-after game fish with a thing of metal or plastic or wood.

Initially, the marine purist was a squidder—a man who used nothing other than a cleverly shaped hunk of block tin, with or without feather-hooked dressing. The squidder remains a classicist, and he is well-represented in today's high surf, but a new aristocrat has arisen: the plugger.

Plugs, contrary to the august International Game Fish Association, confer no special advantage, other than their tendency to draw strikes. Indeed, treble hooks often prove a handicap, because each barb works against another to aid keyholing, a straightening, and ultimate rejection. Often a bass will strike a lure head-on, embedding a forward treble in its mouth, while the plug's tail hook pierces a gill cover. A fish of 20 pounds or more is powerful enough to shake its head and completely straighten one or both of these barbs, even if they are 5/0 heavy-duty types. If hooks hold during this maneuver, the opposing forces involved are likely to create keyholing. Thereafter, if the angler permits any amount of slack, especially during that period when a bass is cartwheeling on the surface, his quarry may eject the lure.

The ability of an angler to cast accurately and then to work his plug or squid with consummate skill is in direct proportion to his success. Any surfman worth his salt is capable of slowing a cast at an opportune moment to drop a lure just beyond an advancing ground swell, and not in front of that moving body of turbulent water. By so doing he insures that the artificial will be swimming in a relatively clear area, and not tumbling in the froth of the breaker.

Top hands not only achieve tack-hole accuracy, they learn to feather spinning-reel spools, or throw the clutch on conventional winches, at that precise moment when forward momentum is nil, the lure poised to touch down. Retrieve begins immediately and speed is gauged to water conditions.

This is an art difficult to teach, since it is achieved only after much trial and error. Accuracy and reflexes that respond to immediate needs cannot be guaranteed by any correspondence school. There is the feel of it, like the feel of a properly cast fly line when a Light Cahill drops exactly right. It is ice skating and skiing and wing shooting—a moment when all things seem to fall right after an extended period of bungling.

Nor is it possible to describe the faculty with which a seasoned surf-caster can absorb the rustle of bait on a pitch-black night, over the boom of breakers and the rush and slide of beach sand. The sights and the sounds are there, distinct over and between other sounds and recollections, but it takes a craftsman to give them their proper places.

How does one reach the beginner? How can he understand the surfman's "black spot," actually an inshore weed bed or shell bar transformed to a darker shade than the surrounding water by the alchemy of polarized lenses? Striped bass frequent black spots, for the weeds and shells harbor bait.

To a beginner, all sea is a succession of crashing combers and wide blue yonder. How can one point out the subtle differences in white water and rip and current that indicate a slough where the great game fish drift in on a flooding tide to devour crabs and other sea creatures? The signs are there, but they are nuances, not neon-lit directions.

I'd like to help, but perhaps it is best this way. Those who would excel will ask questions and seek fine instructors. They will go down to the ocean and walk the sands and ponder the tides. They will become masters of their tackle—a thing necessary if they are to scale the heights of any rod-and-reel sport—and they will then enter the realm of the regulars—the ten percent of anglers who catch ninety percent of the fish.

No bugle ever sounds to vector surfmen into a specific area at a given moment in time, but regulars gather when all of the nebulous clues indicate action. They come striding over the dunes, grotesque in waders and foul-weather parkas, or they arrive in elaborately equipped beach buggies. Often this concentration is triggered by an ideal tidal phase or wind direction; always it follows good fishing on a preceding tide. If bass are here on today's flood, they're likely to be back tomorrow at the same time.

The real pros materialize an hour or so before fish are likely to move in, and they look at the sea. "Good water" is alive and turbulent, but relatively free of suspended sand. A lack of clarity is no handicap, although a lot of sand and debris kicked up by a storm keeps stripers well off shore. "Dirty water" is not a reference to sewage; it refers to storm-torn weeds that discourage the presentation of bait or lure.

The average surfman is fiercely competitive, yet he admires fellow craftsmen. Before the tide is "right," little groups of bewhiskered regulars lounge around the beach buggies, trading shop talk. Always a scattered few explore the surf, hoping to beat bass at their own unpredictable game and find a school on tap prior to the appointed time.

Perhaps thirty minutes before a calculated zero hour, each surfman grabs his long squidding rod, hitches a plug bag higher on one hip, and trudges down into the wash. Each casts methodically, meanwhile searching the sea, the sky, and the competition. It is serious business.

First evidence of bass may be a bent rod etched sharply against the sky somewhere along the picket line. More likely it will be a sudden, sprinkling flurry of small bait which indicates predators below, or even bait washed up by the waves. Of course, any glimpse of a bulging swirl or a quick bomb-burst of white water, which marks a feeding fish, alerts all hands. Wheeling birds insure an immediate stampede of anglers, each striving to be first with a plug on target.

Where sand bars and rock piles lie well off the beach, it often takes a surprisingly long cast to reach feeding fish. A pro swivels, puts back, arms, and legs into one smoothly coordinated motion, and the plug sails eighty to a hundred yards. Duffers backlash, snap their lines, curse, and splash ashore to repair the damage. When this happens, and the lost plug arcs seaward, somebody always yells: "Good cast! Too bad the line wasn't tied to it!"

Thanks to a little-known Law of General Cussedness, a productive bar or rock pile usually lies just beyond a long cast. The solution is to wade far out, until each successive wave becomes a crisis in the making. Sand-beach waders must move constantly, lest the current's gouging action take them down. Where rocks pave the bottom, each will be slippery. Dedicated surfers take frequent cold baths, come up spitting blue-water words—and go right back to work.

Complete success usually depends on tactical skill. If bass are rushing bait on the surface, then a popping plug may best simulate natural forage. Squid, chameleon-like, turn red-amber when they are excited, hence a lure of the same color is most likely to succeed when stripers are slapping them into the air. Frequently an inshore wind defeats the long cast with a plug, and then no lure will prove so deadly as the time-tested tin squid. During the retrieve, each artificial is worked at a speed contrived to match the natural bait in its harried flight from predators. Beginners, lost in the frantic excitement of a blitz, always reel too fast. They get fish, but rarely with the machine-like efficiency of the regular.

No seasoned campaigner shouts with glee as the barbs go home in a thrashing striper. He grunts, leans back, and feels quiet elation rather than panic as line peels off against a preset drag. Rod butt tucked between his legs, the long fiberglass tip bent in a throbbing arc, such a man may stagger to maintain balance as ground swells hit him, but he backs slowly and methodically to the beach. Sometimes a long cast results in an immediate strike. If the bass is big, it may go submarining seaward until all line is gone; then the tip assumes an alarming bend and, finally, there is the sharp report of parting gear. Always there is the thought that this was a true record-breaker.

Enthusiasts speak of "fishing a tide," here defined as about four hours of optimum water conditions. That's a long time in high surf with the wind blowing and combers whacking you in the bread-basket, yet time passes all too quickly in the heat of action. You never feel utter weariness until it is all over and the ocean seems a biological desert and the birds are back on the dunes haggling over stranded bait.

Then the groups gather again to admire fine bass and to tell of the monsters that just kept going, taking line down to a bare spool— and beyond. No striped-bass fisherman in our watery world doubts that he will someday hang a record lineside.

There is much in the high surf that cannot be explained to the uninitiated, but must be experienced. There is cold and high wind and elemental fury. There is failure when sweat and wet are indistinguishable; there are hours of hard labor and broken lines. But there is success as well, triumph in catching truly wild fish. There is satisfaction in challenging the immortal sea and the tides and the roaring combers.

We are going to see much more of this, because America's affluence and modern transportation place the seas within hours of a traveler, regardless of his home base.

Some will go to the plush charter boats, and some to the jetties and the piers. I think it certain that incurable romantics must seek the high surf—where a man faces our last frontier with nothing but a slim wand of fiberglass, a reel, a line, and a lure designed to catch fish-shaped fishes.

# 9

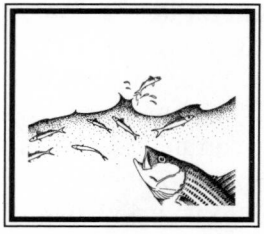

# Striped Bass

*John Cole*

ohn Cole has netted commercially for striped bass from the sand surf using haul seines, an enterprise that occasionally resulted in spectacular numbers of bass, but more often than not, in poor catches or empty tows. In Fish of My Years (1995), Cole tackles an even lower percentage quest, surfcasting for stripers, what he justly describes as "the purest expression of faith."

---

After the war, I went back to Yale just long enough to acquire the standard B.A. That took two accelerated years. We worked a year-round schedule because so many of us veterans had to be educated along with the regular run of undergraduates. There wasn't much time for fishing and I missed it.

Just before Commencement—which I skipped—I got some wonderful news. Peter Matthiessen, my friend and classmate, had told his father I'd be a good captain for the new Fishers Island Country Club launch and his father had followed through with a job offer. As the man responsible for reactivating the Club after its three-year wartime shutdown, Erhard "Matty" Matthiessen had ordered up a brand new,

26-foot Chris-Craft. Powered by two 90-horsepower inboards, the twin screw, trunk cabin boat—all mahogany and gleaming white paint—was one jazzy number. At its controls, I would ferry Club members and guests back and forth across the Sound to Watch Hill, Stonington, New London, Montauk and wherever else they might want to go. My father always told me the contacts I made at Yale would lead to good jobs, but I never imagined they'd be as good as running a boat.

That spring of '48 I'd been to Fishers twice with Peter for weekends. We stayed at his family's summer place, kept the fires going and hung close to the kitchen stove whenever we were indoors. But we spent most of our time on the island's east beaches and along the edges of the rocky coves where Peter said the season's first striped bass would be feeding.

Each of us had a nine-foot, glass surf-casting rod fitted with a level-wind reel loaded with braided Dacron line—an angling innovation that DuPont had developed during the war. We cast Captain Bill's Bluefish Flash At 'Em Poppers, Number 5—a wooden plug the diameter of a broomstick, almost six inches long, fitted with three sets of treble hooks and a hollowed out front end that made a popping sound on the water's surface when you worked it correctly.

There you are, standing on sea-slick, wave-rounded rocks the size of watermelons, the chill sea waters of the northeast's reluctant spring seeping into hip boots pulled from under cellar stairs, swinging your long rod back, back toward the shore then, almost convulsively, arcing it hard toward the sea, the rattling lure pulling line behind it as you lift your blistered thumb from the cold, wet reel. And the lure falls into a faceless sea, so devoid of passion, so gray, so merely there that you know you must bring a kind of madness to sustain you if this is how you will spend your waking hours.

Of all the wondrous variations anglers apply to the simple act of fish catching, surf casting requires the greatest faith. For while every form of angling is, in and of itself, an act of such optimism that it becomes the purest expression of faith, none is more pure than surf casting.

The entire sea lies before you, its elemental vastness underscored by your quite insignificant presence at its edge. You are, indeed, small enough to be swallowed whole should the sea send a swell ashore where you stand so precariously at eternity's rim. One moderate wave, cresting at your shoulders, a sudden foaming at your chest, surging at your waist as it slides so impassively back to its infinite source, carrying you with it as casually as a whale shark sifts plankton from the surface: in that single moment the sea can swallow you without so much as a splash. Yet knowing this is more than a possibility, you persist.

And remarkably so. Because even more than the sea's implacable might, there is its sheer dimension. Not only out, beyond the horizon that is your visual limit of the finite, but down into the depths beyond measure and beyond perception. Yet you stand at the brink of this immeasurable abyss and toss a lure as if you could see its face and know it. You make yourself believe the infinite is not only knowable, but holds a fish in place precisely where you also stand, as if you could stroll to heaven's edge and find a single star waiting for you to carry home.

If there is a measure of such awesome optimism, then it must peak at the point where two young men will wade into the Fishers Island surf and spend entire days and on into dank evenings casting into an utterly barren sea. And for striped bass: a fish known for its finicky refusals, its stubborn unwillingness to be gulled by any lure, if, indeed, there are any stripers within 800 miles of the infinitesimal spot where we stand shielded from such realities by the sheer arrogance of our being.

With those fishless weekends to review—albums without photographs—and with the novelty and pressing pace of my marvelous career as captain, I had no time for further striped bass safaris when I first came back to Fishers that summer. Nor had I much incentive. My patron, benefactor and boss, Matty Matthiessen, reported regularly to me on his unending efforts to catch his first-ever striped bass. All reports were identical: no luck. And not because Matty lacked persistence, or equipment. He owned some of the finest angling accessories on the east coast: all manner of rods, reels, lures and a 12-foot skiff or mahogany and teak that looked as if it had once been a tender aboard J.P. Morgan's yacht, *Corsair*. Powered by a small and silent electric outboard (one of the first) that skiff carried Matty on his ceaseless quest around and along the island's bouldered and tide-swept shores. And each day ended as it began: fishless.

But the stripers were there. That I knew beyond any doubt. I could see them, there among the boulders, 15 feet below the clear, green waters that trembled in the tides just off the point at Fishers east end. Drifting with the tide, leaning out over the launch's stern, I could look down and pick out the dark shapes, striped bass, lying as still as fresh stone, their great heads butted into the current as the fish hung there waiting for whatever morsel the tides might tumble their way.

Matty knew they were there, but he could never fool them. None of the lures he cast or trolled past those dark shapes so charged with the voltage of their stillness was ever mistaken for a tide-borne morsel. Being able to see those fish so clearly and being unable to move them toward a hook became a kind of curse, a terrible penance for wanting to tempt them to violate their undersea sanctity. And each time I saw them, I was reminded that I, too, had yet to hold a striped bass in my hands.

As that splendid summer waxed toward autumn and an end to my captaincy, I began keeping a lightweight casting outfit aboard the launch. In the evenings I'd walk from the dock across the road to the looming country club building—a 1920s stuccoed Tudor excess of four stories tall—and then down the slope to the stony Atlantic shore. To the east along that shore the coast contorted into a series of twisty coves, each hemmed by rising bluffs that pushed almost to the water's edge.

I walked the shore, wading where I had to, soaking my Sperry Topsiders, quite unconcerned about wet khakis. It was that sort of summer. Casting as I went, I'd clamber over boulders until I reached a bluff so steep and rocky that I had to turn back.

A small cove waited just before that barrier, a cove without a beach, little more than a lagoon scooped from the island's rim, as if a giant had pushed down with its thumb. One evening when a sunset sky crimsoned a windless sea, I saw activity on the water's tinted surface as I clambered around the cove's western edge. Swirls and turbulence moved fluently here and there, silent witness to unseen swimmers beneath the gently heaving sea.

The stripers are here, I told myself as I cast a silver plug, many degrees smaller than a Capt. Bill's. On the third cast, a striper hit the plug and was hooked. It seemed so surprisingly easy then, and has ever since. I could have asked, "What's so hard about this?" but I resisted all such dilutions of that moment of glory. Instead, I cranked the reel and in a few minutes the fish lay at my feet in a tide pool there in the boulders.

My first striped bass. And I was one up on Matty, perhaps a seven-pounder, thrashed in the pool's shallows, lying on its side, its silver belly gleaming bright as a new moon.

The strain of tugging it across the shallows had loosened the hooks at the side of its mouth and when I leaned down, holding the rod high in my left hand, the striper shook its head against the line's increased tension and the treble hook pulled loose.

The fish was free. A small sea, pushed by a rising tide, foamed into the cove bringing just enough water to give that bass encouragement and purchase. Its broad tail thrust hard, its head pointed toward the sanctuary of the open sea and the fish, my fish, my first striper, began its escape.

Dropping the rod, I fell to my knees in the water, leaning forward, both hands reaching. The cold, hard muscles of the striper's flanks beat and wriggled against my palms. I raised my arms, tried to get to my feet, my hands extended, gripping my prize.

The fish convulsed, slipped away, fell into the foam, further now from the shore, and vanished.

But I had it in my hands, I told myself. It was a caught fish. It counted. It counted. It had to, I kept saying. I could tell everyone I'd caught my first striper. Or could I?

I cast a few more times, but the fish had moved on. I walked back the rocky trail, soaked, chilled by the wind off the water, stepping carefully in the glowing dark.

Later, I told Peter and Matty. I had to tell someone. They were courteously congratulatory, but I knew the moment was somehow tainted. Where, after all, was the fish? In those days, hook-and-release was scarcely a concept, much less a part of the language.

That summer, that superb, unbridled and altogether delightfully memorable summer, ended with September; although I tried several times, I never hooked another striped bass.

I needn't have felt deprived. In a few years, I would be up to my ass in stripers.

*As an object of sport, for perfect symmetry and beauty of appearance, and as a dish for the table, it is considered only second to the salmon.*

—JOHN J. BROWN,
*The American Angler's Guide,* 1876

# 10

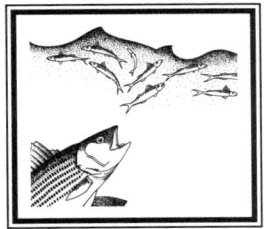

# Gold Medal Fish and Others

Van Campen Heilner and Frank Stick

*S* eabirds are an essential element of the striped bass angler's scene. *Pleasing diversions to watch when the fish aren't hitting—gulls, terns, gannets, and other birds are indispensable aerial sentinels for the presence of surface feeding bass, hovering above the striper schools to pluck panicked baitfish. In this excerpt, from* The Call of the Surf *Stick describes the company of seabirds, the value of gulls in marking fish, and the excitement caused by the sudden and unexpected presence of a school of stripers.*

We were camping on the dunes, where the Inlet cutting through miles of salt meadows has built up a succession of bars, which at low water, the sun shining upon them—as it has a penchant for doing during the fishing season—appear as golden ribbons above the surrounding breakers. This is a justly famous spot for channel bass, and all those lesser fish that love the cuts and inlets. Farther to the south, on the same beach, one could reach in a half hour's walk a shallow point of land jutting into the ocean, and shelving into deep water a hundred feet from shore. Here many a striper had been taken, when conditions were right, and in the autumn at this same spot the blue-fish chased their prey into the undertow.

Shore birds, the little sandpipers and their cousins the yellowlegs, gabbled up and down the beach, and back in the marshes a colony of gulls had raised their broods with an eye no doubt to the excellent fishing so close to hand, and even this late in the season their wild cries sounded throughout the hours of daylight.

The proximity of gulls and terns has always suggested scathers of fish to me, since that first memorable trip to the surf, when ignorant as I was of the habits of seagoing fishes, I cast my bait 'neath where a flock of these birds hovered over the water and immediately hooked a thirty-three-pound channel bass. Since then I have always been temperamentally affected by these roving birds, and a sight of them in any numbers brings an itching to my thumb which only the friction of a rapidly revolving reel can allay. Yes, time and again the gulls have led me to rich treasure of hard-fighting beauties, and time and again, I must confess, they have fooled me into mad dashes up and down the beach, when nought resulted from my efforts. Yet even though the activities of this bird were entirely disassociated from the movements of the fishes, I know that I should still value his companionship on the lone stretches of beach where I pursue my sport.

In each of those varied environments into which my adventuring of the past has led me I have found some feathered creature who seemed to be peculiarly a part of his surroundings, and whose memory I have treasured long after the incidents of that particular trip were forgotten.

I have been thrilled by the soft melody of wood thrush and hermit, as the strains of their melting notes echoed through the depths of forest aisles. I have listened by the hour to the lyric voice of white throat and warbler, and on western bayous the cheery whistle of the cardinal has delighted my ear. And yet the wild, harsh cry of the gull appeals to my senses as strongly as do the finest efforts of these feathered musicians. For there are times and places and certain moods when a man cares most for the bigger, sterner things of life. There is little of melody in the voice of a gull, this I grant you, but there is an individual quality to it, a sort of untamed force which makes it a very part of those vast, wild spaces in which the bird lives his ever-strenuous existence.

Upon the wing he is a strong and steady flier, quick and graceful in all his movements, and untiring in sustained flight, as he needs must be to breast the winds which sweep our coasts. To see a flock of these birds wheeling, darting, and diving into the waves above a school of feeding fish is an inspiring spectacle, and one which will appeal to all who possess a particle of the romance of the wild in their souls.

Yes, I am assured that the gull fits into his environment as well as does the thrush, and the lark, and the cardinal into theirs, and I am convinced, too, that there is as great an inspirational quality in his wild, free cry as can be found in the song of the most gifted woodland warbler.

It was the sight of a flock of gulls hovering and swooping into the waves, close inshore, that drew me from my culinary duties before the open fire one morning during this camping trip I have in mind. The sun had but lately lifted its burnished face above the waters, and in the misty haze that had followed a coolish night objects appeared unreal and evanescent. There was, however, something very real and promising in the clamour which arose from the feeding birds, and with little loss of time I shed the red bandana—the official insignia of the camp chef, and grasping rod and tackle bag, I hurried to the beach. And not a thought did I give to the pots of food which hung above the coals, for what counts scorched food or the cravings of the stomach when fish are feeding in the surf?

When I reached the spot where the gulls were circling, though I peered keenly into the green water, I saw no sign of the fish I sought, and yet that here was a school of mullet on which blues and weakfish love to feed was proven by a reddish patch of considerable extent, which moved slowly through the water some fifty feet from where I stood.

My rod was equipped with a Belmar squid, so I wasted no time in meditation over what manner of fish had attracted my brother fisher-men, the gulls, but made my cast, working the lure rapidly shore-ward. No strike rewarded my efforts, and so again I cast, and yet again without result. And still the gulls darted, swooped, and clam-oured, as though encouraging me to further efforts. On my eighth or tenth cast I varied my system, and on the chance that the fish, what-ever they were, might be cutting into the bait from below, I allowed the squid to sink, and brought it to me with long, jerky movements. Scarce had I taken a dozen turns when there came a mighty strike which swept the tip of my rod downward, the reel handle striking my knuckle a sound crack as it was jerked from my grasp. Out and out my line swept, while with every nerve atingle I pressed hard on the leather drag and braced back against the rod. A hundred, two hundred, three hundred feet of line the fish took ere he halted his rush, and swam parallel to the beach. I felt sure that another besides a blue, or else a monster specimen of this hard-fighting species had fastened to my squid, and I played him carefully. Fifteen or twenty minutes of battle he gave me ere I had him close inshore, and then as he lifted into a curling breaker, with the sun shining greenly through, I made him out. A good striped bass he was, and long before I had succeeded in coaxing him into a wave which laid him gently at my feet I had raised such a to-do that my two friends, aroused at last from their slumbers, joined me, a bit shy as to clothing but fully equipped with rods and tackle.

Five bass, ranging up to eighteen pounds in weight, we took from this school in the space of an hour, and then the fish moved onward, and the gulls with them, and we returned to camp for a belated though doubly relished breakfast.

*The striper does not have the raw power of moonshine whiskey. He is more like a fine Bordeaux. He is a fish to savor, to sip, to taste and to learn. He is not a fish that can be caught on a fly rod, he is a fish that should be. The striper, like the trout, takes just a little more time.*

—J. Kenney Abrames,
*Striper Moon*, 1994

# 11

# The Shining Tides

Win Brooks

T he Shining Tides *(1952) by Win Brooks is the only successful novel based on the striped bass. Set in Cape Cod, it involves several forms of striper fishing, a good deal of striped bass lore, a charter boat business, a nighttime poaching scheme for stripers, a romance, and the precarious existence of a great old bass called* Roccus. The Shining Tides *also includes a character named Judge Wickett, a non-angler who is serendipitously exposed to striper fishing. Judge Wickett's subsequent birth as a striped bass angler is a classic portrayal of a fisherman completely and helplessly ensnared by the sport.*

---

Judge Wickett's summer began auspiciously with beautiful weather. There was early July heat but his estate was situated to take advantage of the prevailing southwest breeze. To the somewhat restricted summer colony of which he was the recognized leader the persons he best liked and admired had returned. Here, as in all the circles of his professional and social life, he was respected, looked up to for guidance, held up as the shining example of integrity, a man who practiced privately the stern code of morals he publicly enunciated from the bench—the very soul of honor.

He quickly relaxed from the strain of adjudicating issues involving man's freedom or imprisonment, his life or death. He played golf regularly at Dunetrap, where he was chairman of membership, and made two early trips to Oyster Harbors and Eastward Ho. He sailed in the yacht club's week-end races, paid a friendly call on Father O'Meara, walked the dunes a good deal with his daughter and grandson, joined the colony picnics, swam regularly.

A New York contractor, a Boston insurance broker and a marine artist were his regular golf companions. They were a high-handicap quarter which never fired the course. Originally they had played dime Nassau and engaged in other small wagers, but this practice had been discontinued the previous summer at the Judge's request because he had presided over a trial at which the moral code of the public with relation to anti-gambling statutes had been raised in issue by counsel for a notorious bookmaker, who had contributed heavily to the campaign funds of at least two elected state officers. Defense counsel had suggested naively in final argument to the jury that perhaps even His Honor had, at one time or another during his exemplary life, been a party to a transgression of the hypocritical law that permitted wagering at race tracks and forbade it elsewhere.

On the fairway, although his drives often strayed, the Judge pursued an objective course within the boundaries of the rules, calling penalty strokes on himself sometimes to the annoyance of his partner, the broker, who was given to taking his score a little more seriously. During the first game of the summer the Judge played and won two holes before discovering that he was playing a lost ball, and these holes he insisted upon forfeiting though none but himself could have been aware of the mistake.

He was a fair sailor though not a dusty one, given to taking few chances. The *Sailfish* was too wet for him but he managed one or another of the smaller one-man or two-man crew classes. In the windward position he never gave way in a luffing match, but on the other hand he never tried to jockey out of position a boat which had the right of way. He did little maneuvering while awaiting the starting gun, being content to cross the line with the trailers, who used no stop watches. Sailing alone in the second meet of the summer, he scored a rare victory due to an unexpected offshore slant of wind, but he reported disqualification, having fouled the turning buoy.

"Tried to jibe, should have known better," he called over to the judge's boat at the finish.

There had been no official boat at the rounding mark and no competition nearby. The yachting reporter for one of the Boston papers dwelt on the incident, and the same paper subsequently carried a brief, trite editorial evaluating sportsmanship and honesty.

Judge Wickett wasn't an angler and didn't expect to be one. Certain of the yacht club crowd had tried on occasion to convert him. These were, in his subconscious estimate, the slightly less desirable members of the colony who drank a little too much on regatta days and fished all night after the sailing. In response to their importunities he said he was getting along in years—though he was in fact younger than many of them—and fishing was too much like work. Moreover, he couldn't seem to get excited about any of its prospects.

Striped-bass fishermen, the Judge had observed, lived more on hope than realization. They lost sleep and were likely to be boors. They exaggerated, both about the size and number of fish caught and those they just missed catching. They were, of course, fine sportsmen and completely trustworthy about everything except fishing. They were far from trustworthy as regards the location of fish taken and lures used to take them, and some were not above changing lures to misguide late arrivals.

"Anyone who fishes places his reputation on the block," he observed to an angling golfer—and that was still his opinion this daybreak of waning July when he looked down from the master bedroom of his fieldstone house to the long reach of shore and dunes emerging from half-light into what promised to be a beautiful day. Terns were working, their discordant cries alive with hunger. The tide was close to flood. It was an hour when, with none on the beach, he enjoyed a dip. He would, as was his custom, swim approximately fifty yards parallel with the beach and not over his depth. He'd float on his back, kicking his feet for a minute or so, duck again and run up to the house, where, after a warm-to-cold shower and a once-over shave, he would breakfast on orange juice, black coffee, one slice of dry toast and a three-minute egg.

He felt vibrant. He pulled on the khaki shorts he used for swimming and thrust his feet into old sneakers from which the laces had been removed. Quietly, so as not to disturb Sue and Andrew, he went downstairs and, in a little dogtrot because he felt so good, to the sand.

Approaching the near jetty he observed without annoyance that his favorite swimming spot was in use by a fisherman whose presence he had not observed from his window. He decided to swim a few hundred feet beyond the angler, where a sandy point thrust from a headland into the bay. His course took him through thatch grass behind the fisherman where, he noted, a sedan with a New York license plate had been parked at the foot of a wooded road. This was his own property but he did not post it, and anyone of good behavior was welcome to use it.

The angler was a heavy, tanned man about the Judge's age. He had a full head of iron-gray hair and an energetic thrust of belly above a pair of blue shorts, his only attire. He was bottom-fishing with bait, using two rods, one of which he set in a sand spike after making a long cast. As the Judge watched, he baited a second hook with sea worms and walked down the beach about fifty feet to make a second cast beyond the lazy lift of rollers. Then he walked up to his knees into the curl of surf and stood waiting with the rod butt between his legs.

The Judge called, "Good morning! Any luck?" This was a question which, without having any interest in the answer, he invariably asked all fishermen.

The angler half-turned his head to show an unshaved jut of chin and said, "How in hell could I have any luck when I just started?" The unexpected answer brought a smile to Judge Wickett—a reasonable enough reply based on logic, he thought.

"Any bass around this dump?"

"Why, I've seen bass caught in that very spot," said the Judge. "I'm not a fisherman myself."

"You're not, huh?" All the disdain of the zealot for the unbeliever was in the three words.

The angler lifted his rod tip and retrieved a few feet of line. The Judge was about to pass along when the other grunted like a rhinoceros, set back on the rod and shouted, "By the Jesus, they're here!"

Then he began a variety of contortions which entranced Judge Wickett. He backed up onto the beach, reeling like mad. He raced down into the water up to his hips. He backed up again and ran along the beach. His rod, tip high, arced toward the surface and his line made a sizzling sound cutting the water. "Big son of a bitch!" he shouted.

"Well, good luck to you," the Judge called. Though his curiosity was aroused, chiefly by the other's antics, he was still not sufficiently interested to remain and watch the outcome. He had started to pass along when he became aware of a steadily burring click below him and, glancing down, he saw the second rod jerking violently in the sand spike, line whipping off the reel.

"See here!" he called. "You have a fish on your other rod."

The angler half-turned to shout over his shoulder, "Well, grab it and sink the hook in the bastard!"

The Judge involuntarily started down the beach, then stopped.

"I can't do that. I never handled a rod, never caught a fish."

"You grab that goddamn rod and fast, or by the Jesus, when I beach this fish I'll chew your ass out!"

This was one of the few times the Judge had been profanely addressed and certainly the first time in his life anyone had ever threatened to chew his ass out. He was more than mildly startled. Then, not under duress, wishing merely to be helpful, he hurried to the free rod, lifted it from the holder and felt life pulling distantly and viciously at the line.

"Set the son of a bitch! Jerk back on him!"

The Judge jerked back, felt the heavy tug, felt a line burn across two fingers of his left hand.

"Hook the bastard? Good. Snap off the click and tighten up the drag."

Judge Wickett had not the slightest idea how to snap off the click and tighten the drag, but after experimenting with the handle and the axle nut he finally threw out the click and the screaming ceased.

"The drag, goddamn it—the drag! Turn down on that little star thing on the right side under the handle. Turn it away from you."

The Judge, working under these instructions, suddenly felt the rod take terrific strain, nearly tear from his grasp.

"Loosen up on the drag, goddamn it. Not so tight. You'll pop that line."

The Judge loosened up. The distant fish ran parallel with the outside rollers. The Judge moved into the water, following. In a few minutes he was up to his waist and the fish was close to the end of the jetty.

The angler called, pumping his own fish, "Don't let the son of a bitch get around those rocks; he'll cut the line. Tighten up and turn him!"

The Judge tightened up, felt the tail rap on the line. Within him an excitement awoke. His arms ached. The bass stopped a few feet from the jetty and turned back. The Judge felt an exultation. "Turned him!" he yelled.

"Well, keep the son of a bitch clear of my line."

The battle lasted about fifteen minutes. The Judge, mortally engaged, was aware when the other backed up on the beach lifting his silver trophy on a wave crest, beaching him. He was aware a short time later that the other stood behind him.

"Here—take over," he gasped.

The other backed away. "Not on your obscene life! Go to work on him. Tighten up a little more, he's tiring."

The Judge went to work on him. He discovered that by properly adjusting the drag, lifting the rod tip and dropping it fast while reeling, he could pump the fish closer as it tired. He saw the bass roll green inside the rollers. He reeled like mad.

"Now back up on the beach! Take the bastard easy. Not too fast! Not too fast! Lift him in the wave and I'll grab the leader. That's it! That's it! Goddamn!"

The fish was dragged to the dry sand, its life all but ebbed. The Judge, perspiring, his hands trembling, his blood pumping faster than it had in many a day, walked over to inspect the prize. The angler dispatched it with one rap of a loaded club. It lay gleaming silver-green, a beautiful fish, with bluish-brown stripes darkening.

"Nice goin', kid," said the angler. Nice fish you got there. Bigger 'n mine. Weigh more than twenty pounds."

"Is that all!" the Judge exclaimed. "I thought he must weigh forty at least. He looks more than you estimate."

"They're deceiving. But he fought like a son of a bitch, didn't he?"

"Like a son of a bitch!" said Judge Leander Wickett. It was a phrase he hadn't used since his college years.

"Well, we'll bait up and cast out again. May be a big pod of fish in this hole."

The angler baited both rods, cast one. The weighted rig described a parabolic arc and splashed distantly. "Go ahead, cast out."

"I might break something, you know. I'd prefer you to."

"Christ's little kittens! Here, let me show you. Right thumb here. Be sure the reel is on free spool. Take it back easy like this. . . . Now forward quickly with just a little snap of your right wrist. Don't move your left arm. . . . No, not that way. Jesus and all hands around!"

The Judge had moved adequately, but had not kept sufficient thumb pressure on the unspooling line, and the result was a grandfather of backlashes and a ten-foot cast. The angler unraveled the bird's nest to an accompaniment of words not often heard in a courtroom. He again demonstrated form and the Judge responded.

"Now you're cooking. Haul in and try it again."

The Judge, cooking, showed definite improvement.

"Okay, let it lay out there. Hit hard if a fish picks it up."

The new excitement did not diminish. The Judge fished for an hour longer, twice changing bait. He was taut with the expectation of a strike and tense with the memory of his battle with his first striper. It was the angler who finally suggested that, tide having turned, it was probably useless to fish longer in daylight. The Judge helped his companion carry the rods and fish to the car.

"Hey, that's your fish, kid."

"Oh, no," said the Judge. "It was your equipment. It's your fish." He wanted to say that he didn't want the bass, but that would be a misrepresentation—he wanted it like he wanted his right arm.

"Hell, you caught it. I never took another man's fish yet."

So Judge Wickett let himself be argued into it. He introduced himself by name only. The other responded: "My name's Popowski. Got a junk yard in Brooklyn."

They arranged to meet and fish the following morning, and the Judge started home with his fish. He was vaguely disappointed that he met no one on the beach, but the colored maid, rolling her eyes, greeted him with enthusiasm.

"What do you think of that? Caught him myself."

He went to the foot of the stairs.

"Oh, Sue—Andrew! Come down and I'll show you really something."

His daughter came down in her robe, his grandson in his pajama bottom. The Judge held his prize aloft, his fingers, cut, in its gills. The fish dripped blood on the rug.

"Oh, boy!" said Andrew.

"Well, Dad! Who caught that?"

"I caught it," said the Judge. "Caught it myself. Man, regular fellow, Pop-something—runs a junk yard—let me use his rod."

"What's he weigh, Gramp? Fifty pounds maybe, huh?"

The Judge was tempted to let the estimate go uncorrected—merely state that he didn't know—but that ingrained sense of integrity brushed temptation aside; there must be integrity in angling as in all else.

"Oh, no, Andrew. Perhaps twenty pounds, twenty-one. Not more. But he fought like a son of a bitch."

"Dad!"

"Sorry." He was genuinely grieved and amazed at himself. "I'm awfully sorry. But he did fight like the very devil. Vicious fish—courageous." There was a new gleam in his eye.

In such fashion Judge Leander Wickett of the Massachusetts Superior Court became a convert to the art of the angler. By evening the entire summer colony was aware he had caught a twenty-pound striper and planned to fish next day with a companion who, through some transition not of the Judge's making, had assumed the social and financial stature of a steel tycoon from New York.

The Judge moved that day into the circle of the veteran bass addicts whose company he had rather studiously avoided in years past. He listened to their fishing stories, told his own. Joe Hartley, a night caster, invited him along some evening and he accepted gratefully, though he knew Joe always had a bottle in his plug bag. His day was full of discussion of rods, glass blanks, reels, the merits of a wide spool, nylon and linen lines, popping plugs, underwater plugs, wagtails, block tin, barracudas, butt harnesses, gaffs, sand spikes. The zealots welcomed him with open arms and hymns. Merely because he felt exalted, uplifted, he sipped two Manhattans instead of his usual one before lunch. He went to the golf club but excused himself from his foursome on the ground that his arms ached and he must save his strength for possible battle the next morning.

Before night he had put through a phone call to a New York sporting goods house, ordering an expensive assortment of tackle to be shipped air express to Hyannis, where he would pick it up. In the evening, seated on his veranda and reliving in memory the dramatic fight of the morning, he received a visit from Clem Hartley, Joe's brother. Clem was generally recognized as a hot bass fisherman. His wife was known as the Striped-Bass Widow, which is worse than being a golf widow because golfers sleep at night, as a rule. Clem had heard he had caught a bass and was calling to congratulate him. The Judge recounted the circumstances for at least the tenth time.

"Good fish, they tell me," Hartley said.

"Twenty pounds or so," said the Judge.

"Weigh him?"

"No. The man whose rod I used estimated the weight."

"They're hard to guess. Fool you, unless you've been at it a long time. Look heavier than they are, most of them. Care to show me?"

The Judge led him to the kitchen. He felt a misgiving lest, in Hartley's opinion, the fish would weigh less than twenty pounds and he would be placed in the position of having misjudged or exaggerated. The maid had cleaned and gilled it for baking and, in the freezer, the Judge thought his fish appeared smaller. But Hartley said, "Better than twenty when he was caught. Closer to twenty-two."

Judge Wickett felt better, but when Clem had gone he realized he had talked too much about the fish all during the day, probably boring a lot of polite people who hadn't the slightest interest. He determined to watch out in the future—let his fish speak for themselves.

Next day he caught no fish. The tycoon of rusted steel departed Brooklyn-ward, his vacation ended. The day following, in the same hole, fishing alone, the Judge hooked a big fish and lost it. He made no mention of this to anyone. His tackle arrived and he spent hours testing it out, casting various lures from the beach, learning to give action to them. He caught a small bass on a plug, took another night-fishing with Jeff Hartley. He played only one round of golf during the last week of July. He didn't sail in the week-end racing, but joined the anglers in the rocking-chair fleet as they talked their preparations for night excursions. He ordered a fourteen-foot lapstreak skiff and a five-horsepower outboard motor. He put his golf clubs away in a closet. He was a goner.

*The unseen quarry and mysterious dark water, the pleasure taken in the strong and skillful cast, the sound and smell of sea and weather, the healing solitude, and the suspense, are reward enough to the true sportsman who seeks no profit from his hobby, and surfcasting for striped bass probably claims more fanatics than any other form of saltwater fishing.*

—PETER MATTHIESSEN,
*Men's Lives*, 1986

# 12

# Slaughter at Pochet Hole

### Frank Daignault

ᒧ n the surf, most outstanding catches of striped bass occur at night, the best surfcasters becoming supremely adept at fishing in darkness. But nothing electrifies the senses of a bass angler as much as a daytime 'blitz', a rare experience in which stripers in the shallows can not only be felt on the rod, but also seen in the waves. The blitz is to the surfcaster as the great hatch is to the trout angler—a heedless feeding frenzy, the confluence and combustion of predator and prey, that highlights a season. In Slaughter at Pochet Hole (1976), Frank Daignault records the moments of an almost legendary striper blitz in Cape Cod surf.

---

On Cape Cod's Nauset Beach, where the back trail cuts east to meet the open surfline, a bowl-shaped impression, known as Pochet Hole, has been dug into the beach by wind and tide. It looks like a good place if you've never fished Nauset, but to me it's one of the stiffest spots on Cape Cod. One regular once went a whole season without a good fish. And there is a saying among the beach-buggy regulars that it will produce if you wait long enough. Yet they always add that only a fool would wait when ten more miles of sand would put him into fish.

Pochet Hole is easy. Because of this, people seeking a variety of forms of recreation find their way to this most accessible spot. It is popular with bathers who come out in four-wheel-drive vehicles for the day. It is the choice of a score of anglers equipped with self-contained RV vehicles who baitfish with seaworms. It is a spot that must be passed by all the surfmen to Nauset on Sunday when they leave the beach. This was a Sunday, the first in August.

Our family safari was made up of my wife Joyce, our oldest son Dick, who is fourteen; Carol, age 12, and our ten-year-old twins, Susan and Sandra. We were all equipped to cast plugs, Dick and I preferring to use conventional gear.

We were leaving the beach passing Pochet about noon, planning to work another spot on the next night. Due to the fact that there is little surf fishing done with any success in the daytime, we've learned to do our travelling in the heat of day to save our nights for fishing. As we drove by, a large gallery of spectators encircled an angler who was fighting a bluefish and we stopped to watch. We couldn't help but notice the amount of bait there.

Huge shoals of blueback herring discolored the bowl to gray. For all but the 100-foot wide opening on the seaward side, the bluebacks were confined within the bars that encircled them. It almost seemed as if they knew that certain death waited for them on the outside. As we watched, at least for those moments, the baitfish went unmolested.

After the angler landed his bluefish we asked if there had been any number of fish. From his description, blues had twice swept in to chop at the herring for a few minutes and then withdrawn to deeper water. We readied wire leaders for the impending third pass.

With blues, the hands-down choice is always a popping plug and the few fish caught before we arrived had been taken on the surface. We had made our choice because were thinking about blues—not the bait. Only a bluefish would hit a squid-simulating lure amid an acre of herring. When the third pass came my surface popper was bouncing just outside the bait when it was engulfed by a bluefish. As I fought the blue, the bowl cracked wide open.

Huge sheets of baitfish glistened in unison leaping hundreds at a time and clear, round, empty spots appeared looking from a distance like pock marks in what had been an undisturbed herd. As the killers tore through the bluebacks, I could see that it wasn't the dark forms of bluefish so familiar to us but rather the light tan, almost bronze, of stripers. And they were big! The sight of them was a mild shock. Somehow what I had seen caught had ruled out the possibility that both gamefish could be there. The attack ended suddenly, and the bait regrouped without a single striper taken.

Dick and I hurriedly dug out small, blue swimming plugs that we felt would best imitate the bluebacks and the girls clipped them to wire leaders. Now that we were armed with lighter, harder to cast swimmers, reaching the strike zone posed more of a problem than when we had been using poppers. Having noticed a tendency for both gamefish to come through the opening taking only the bait from the seaward side, we waded out onto one of the bars in order to improve our position for the next eminent kill.

It was then that we experienced one of the most pleasant, most astounding sights of our fishing lives. We saw stripers—big stripers. I've seen them hundreds of times before, busting or rolling or twisting their bodies through the surf after bait. But never until that day had I stood among them to watch them cruise by like pets. First, one long, dark form; then three; and then we gasped as a wave of fish passed so close that the motion of a shaky, backlashed cast flushed them out of sight. Not small fish like those we often catch; these were all logs and there were many!

I've always thought that I was familiar with the movements of striped bass—an intimacy develops out of a lifetime of mid-watch hunts, where you feel your way seeking them out, plugging here, then there, until the hit comes. After a while the pieces seem to fall together. Maybe, for a given spot, it is when the water begins to flow with force; perhaps behind a favorite sand-bar at slack high; or a given point near deep water where you think, or suspect there must be, an ocean current. You put the good nights down in your log and when these nights begin to have common conditions you've learned something. Sometimes you can come back to a spot after religious entries in your log and pull it off—sometimes not. Nonetheless, you *think* that you have an intimacy with stripers. Back to that day in August.

With these fish it seemed that there was a certain organization to it all. Not that we could dope out how they were doing it, but the results were evident. They had the bait where they wanted it—trapped in a cache of sand and sea—seeming to be executed far too efficiently to be dismissed in our minds as a mere accident. Some fish would scurry over the bar we fished from, as if their turn to kill had come.

Others, always a larger group, slid more slowly, more parallel to the bar, as if they were assigned as guards for this precious find. It was as though they saw, or had experienced before, the fruits of good organization, with some fish assigned the task of confining the bluebacks, while their comrades feasted. In no case did the bass ever drive the bait seaward. The bluefish, however, were the renegades.

The blues moved through the surf with more speed, seeming more excited, darting about recklessly, scattering the bluebacks and working singularly from every direction; one passed so close that when he turned, his tail whipped the boy's waders. I cursed as one took my plug and while I fought him, blanket-size pods of bait made good their escape. Some of the bluefish had gone over the bar cutting huge shoals of bluebacks from the main school, forcing them out into open water. The heat mounted.

Dick's drag was groaning and he turned long enough to tell me he had a good bass, but I had to leave him to remove the blue, which was about eight pounds. On my way back out I noticed the lad's fish on the gaff as he sloshed through the surf in triumph. I trembled as I cast among the shadows of the huge fish that coasted past at a leisurely pace in only three feet of water. One striper, of about 40 pounds or more, rose toward my plug and at the instant when I thought he would take it, he turned and joined the others. For all the fish we could see, there was little interest in the lures we offered. As the boy and I directed our casts to these "cows," our frustration mounted. Not that we were alone; the other anglers were drawing a blank with their surface plugs as well. It occurred to us at about the same time to fish blind, disregarding those stripers we could see—a feat calling for considerable resignation.

When we did, we hooked up almost simultaneously, grinning at one another. Apparently, and I'll never quite be sure of this, those stripers that we could see *could see us*. When we turned to blind casting, we benefited from the cover of distance. It might have been that there were more stripers farther out—I don't know. At any rate, three more stripers and another blue were beached by us, not without the attention of 10 or 15 other casters who had spread around us at comfortable distances. They were wearing bathing suits and using surface plugs. More about them later.

On the beach, at about the center of the hole, a good crowd had gathered fishing feverishly. I worried about my wife and our three daughters who could never let a blitz pass without using the surf rods mounted on the front of our beach-buggy. We felt compelled to check on them—we ran.

When we reached the group it was pandemonium. Anglers were spread for 300 feet, casting like mad and the bluebacks were taking a whipping in the first wave. In contrast to the guarding fish on the outside, these, that tore through the surf, had come in hungry. There wasn't a swimming plug in the line, except those that the girls were throwing and they had found their mark.

Both our twin daughters backed up the beach as their spinning rods arched from stripers. I was in the midst of giving Sandra help with the gaff, when I turned in time to see a surfman go down to help Susan with her fish. Just as the lineside was in the first wave, apparently ready, he grabbed the line in an effort to help her and it broke.

When I hauled Sandra's fish up onto the beach, which was over 20 pounds, I noticed Irish pennants of monofilament trailing from her plug. Certain that it was no knot of mine, I asked her about it.

"I had to tie the plug on," she said. "I lost the other when a man tried to help me land my fish."

Apparently, and we pieced this together later, two different casters that day, however well meaning their intentions, had grasped lines up tight with good fish in this heavy Cape Cod surf just before the lines broke.

It was still a swinging scene. I turned and gaffed a good fish for a guy and heard the report of parting mono somewhere from the crowd. About 100 feet to the right, big stripers were cutting through the first wave and my wife and I saw a fish that was easily the largest striper we've ever laid eyes on. When I cast for him, a fish that later weighed 32 pounds inhaled the plug and he *wasn't* the one. While I fought him, a guy beside me called:

"What am I doing wrong?"

I threw him a swimmer which I never saw again.

In that same flurry, I hooked a striper that went out over the bar taking a good 150 yards of line but I dropped him. I loaned my gaff to a man that was begging for it; Dick took another fish; we heard another line break; my wife Joyce caught a blue that later weighed over 16 pounds; and our twins sprawled on the high beach from exhaustion. People were running all over the place and the gang in bathing suits, out on the bar, had abandoned it.

Still wearing Polaroids, the boy and I went out on the bar and the monsters were still there. I'll spare you the details of every strike in an effort to be brief, suffice it to say the lad and I took three more—one weighing 43 pounds.

It was sunset before the smoke of Pochet cleared and the four children and I had all put stripers on the beach over 30 pounds. Mom had spent so much time helping the girls and watching over them that she had really done very little fishing. However, she still felt good about her blue.

"Watching those girls with fish on," she said, "is more fun than fishing anyway."

Reflecting upon that day at Pochet, its Indian name now holds a certain mystique in all our minds. For each of us indelibly pressed in our memories, are the myriad of highlights that continually punctuated the afternoon. As a family, we stood side by side sharing the joy of it all. As individuals, each recalls the feel of a good fish and the elation of putting some on the beach. Together, it is a memory of blue and white glistening from the August sun yet fanned for comfort by the coolness of the summer sou'west. And every time we pass the spot a quiet, almost reverent twinge grips us. The twins press their noses to the glass; Carol chatters incessantly about her 35-pounder; Dick scans the water as if he were all business; and Mom and I turn our heads from the trail long enough to give the surf there the knowing look of an old friend.

# 13

# The Surf

Russell Chatham

*J n the days when San Francisco Bay still held an abundance of striped bass, a portion of the stock would venture past the Golden Gate Bridge to spill north and south along the open California coast. For some time, striper angling in this tumultuous habitat was the exclusive province of fishermen who wielded long plug casting rods. One morning, Russell Chatham delivered a yellow streamer to a willing fish behind a breaker, taking the first striped bass ever on a fly rod in the Pacific Ocean. Recounted in* Striped Bass on the Fly *(1977).*

Bolinas lies dark and silent under a tenebrous curtain of fog which shrouds the Mesa and presses against the steep ridge of Mt. Tamalpais. Summer, before daylight: A dim street lamp fails to brighten the end of wharf road where the old wooden bulkhead seeps and drips, a curious dog wanders a slow zigzag among several cars from which the vague forms of men emerge.

Words are exchanged but not overheard as the falling tide hisses steadily at the jetty and the surf crashes against the beach only yards away. Beyond, barely visible, beach, waves and sky are deep gray, hinting at the rich chiaroscuro of a later hour.

There is the thud of waders on the ground, and trunk lights reveal massive tackle boxes, foul weather gear and gaff hooks. Powerful ten-foot surf rods are being assembled, some with spinning reels, others with squidders. It is almost time.

I cinch the wader straps and pull on a rain parka, tying it tightly at the waist. I feel slightly foolish when I pick up my fly rod and examine the fly that looked so big at home. I am standing near a man whose rod is exactly three times as thick as mine and his lure, dangling from the first guide, is as large as my forearm. I consider for a moment getting back in the car and going home.

At a point determined the previous morning, I wade into the breakers. To my left the channel runs like a monstrous river rapid into the surf which doubles in height to curl over it. A wave hits me from the front, breaking over my head. Some of it goes inside the parka. The three other surf fishermen have waded far out and I notice they jump when a wave approaches. I realize that if I turn sideways first, then jump, this gives better stability.

It is getting light and no fish appear. I have spent perhaps an hour casting and moving around, trying to see what I can and can't do with a fly line in the breakers. Suddenly one of the surfmen snaps his rod upwards and is on a fish.

At nearly the same instant a sea pigeon veers in front of me, diving into a smooth trough between the waves. There is an awesome boil and several stripers scatter a school of anchovy like fireworks.

I wade as deeply as I dare, holding loops of monofilament coiled in my mouth. Line and fly trail back toward the beach until I spot an anchovy skipping through a hollow. Rolling the thick nylon head forward then tightly back, I drop the longest cast I can behind the next breaker. There will be a six- or seven-second retrieve before the next wave engulfs everything in foam.

Two seconds is all it takes for the strike. I lose control of the line as it vanishes alarmingly toward the Farallon Islands. It is a terribly long run, close to a hundred yards, clearly the farthest of any striped bass I'd ever hooked.

But after that, the fight is routine with the bass sawing back and forth in the breakers. Once, I see him swimming in the curl of a wave which is like the window of an aquarium. Then he is on the sand and I have his jaw.

Up on the beach I put him down and marvel at his deep green back and vivid stripes. The yellow fly shines like a light from the corner of his mouth. I am looking at the first striped bass ever caught in the Pacific Ocean on a fly.

*He puts up a long dogged fight and when at last a wave lays him at your feet there probably never was a fish fresh from the salt that give you a bigger thrill. Days of heaving into the breakers, nights of standing in the shifting sands of the undertow, have all been repaid.*

—Van Campen Heilner,
*Salt Water Fishing*, 1937

# 14

# Shallow Water Stripers

### Phil Schwind

N o aspect of the recent evolution of fly-fishing for stripers has excited anglers as much as sight-fishing for them on broad sand flats flooded by clear ocean waters. In this northern equivalent of bonefishing, skittish bass, often of large size, are stalked while wading, or are caught from poled, shallow-draft skiffs. This vignette from Cape Cod Fisherman (1974) takes a look at very early flats fishing for striped bass long before it reached its present popularity and refinement.

---

For years Harris and I and the fleet generally had watched stripers in shallow water on the Brewster Flats. While *Whitecap* was not as handy in shoal water as *Nonny*, that shoal-water fishing I knew, and *Whitecap* carried me there. I came ashore one day, frustrated and tired.

"Are there any stripers around?" asked Freddy MacFarlane in the Goose Hummock Shop, the local tackle shop.

"Tens of thousands," I said, "on the Brewster Flats. It's like a goldfish bowl; you can look at them but you can't catch them."

I hadn't meant the statement for the press, it was a mere statement of fact, but I was quoted the next day in the *Boston Herald* in Henry Moore's "Rod and Gun" column.

Bob Pond, who made the Atom Plug and later successors, said, "If the fish are there I can catch them."

We made a deal. "If you can catch one fish, I'll give you the trip for free because I will have learned something. If I can show you ten thousand fish, by your own count, and you can't catch one, then you owe me sixty dollars worth of plugs."

He came the next day and gave me more than sixty dollars worth of plugs, win, lose, or draw. It was a trip neither he nor I will ever forget. The day was perfect for sighting fish; flat calm, the tide starting to drop at noon when the sun was right overhead. He and a buddy, Art Posgay, and Bill Fitzpatrick of the Massachusetts Department of Natural Resources (who was along because I had seen nine-inch stripers, something new for these waters) coasted out of the harbor. We sped to the Brewster Flats, where I slowed down. Bob and his partner started to cast off the stern while I was still under way.

"You're wasting your strength, fellows," I said, "I can see every inch of the bottom and there are no fish here." Then I nudged Bill. "See that patch of rough water over there, a quarter of a mile south? That's stripers."

"No," whispered Bill, "that's a wind slick."

"You think I don't know stripers when I see them? That's a school of fish."

We crept down on the rough water. It was a quarter-mile-long school of big stripers, thirty- to forty-pounders, finning, as they were wont to do in the shallow water of Brewster Flats at that time of year. I said casually to Bob and his partner, "You want to see a few stripers? Put down your rods and come up forward."

They came, they looked, they scrambled back frantically for their rods and we got closer and closer. I shut off and coasted close to the school. Bob and his friend cast and cast, surface plugs and swimmers, big plugs and small, red plugs and blue. The fish were not feeding and simply turned out of the way of the plugs.

"Here," I said, "I can get fish to follow a plug—which you obviously can't do. Let me show you." I jogged easily ahead until we came to a new school of big fish, fish that hadn't been alerted by Bob's frantic casting. The fish were all easing lazily nor'west with the tide, their dorsal fins and the tips of their tails showing above the surface. I popped a surface plug just astern of the last fish's tail and exploded it. I made all the commotion in the water I could with that one plug. Every fish in the school turned to follow it. I cranked and popped, cranked and popped all the way to the boat with the whole school following curiously. Not one fish tried to bite my lure. When my plug reached the boat and I had to lift it out of the water the fish turned away, not scared, just not hungry and not particularly interested.

"Come," I said, "west of here are slightly smaller fish. Sometimes they bite better. And west of them are still smaller fish, schoolies; sometimes they will bite when the big ones won't."

Bob said, "You sound like a fish market; big one here, medium-size ones next to them, and little ones at the end of the counter." But that's the way it was: So constantly we lived with the fish, we knew their habits well. Finally, after the turn of the tide, when the wind sprang up and ruffled the surface of the water, Bob's partner managed, with my coaching, to catch one lone fish, a twenty-five-pounder. Neither he nor Bob ever quite got over that day, though they fished with me for years afterwards.

# 15

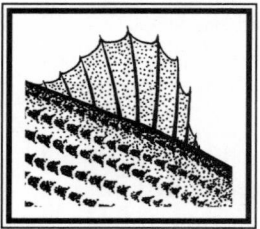

# Hudson River Portraits

*John Bryan*

---

*n Hudson River Portraits (1978), John Bryan underscores one of the chief virtues of striped bass—their great accessibility as an inshore game fish, even to the urban angler. No other temperate species is found over as great a variety of coastal habitats, both natural and manmade, such that it is possible to combine a brief lunch break or an after-dinner foray with the appropriate tide at a beach, sea wall, bridge, or jetty, and if fortune allows, hook a specimen weighing tens of pounds. Flyrodder Bryan writes of mastering his local "beat", a stretch of the Hudson River along Manhattan, his efforts culminating in an epic battle with an outsized striper.*

---

The night was special with anticipation. I had unlocked the secrets of the river's trophy fish, and the morrow would find me fast into a great one, or two, or three. The years of catching throwbacks were over, a new time was to begin for me. My home pool was about to become exotic. With dawn, my private, singly fished beat would see a new master.

New York City's Hudson River is polluted, its fauna are infested with every conceivable chemical poison, its shores are awash with garbage, its infrequent human visitors are not the clientele of the Restigouche. But the Manhattan Hudson is a short amble from my 112th Street Columbia University apartment. And I have learned to probe its thick depths.

I had been fishing the uptown Hudson there at 116th Street for three years. A shortage of time had forced me to try the local water. Catskill, Adirondack, and even Watershed outings were scarce and generally unavailable. But I must frequent the feel of the rod, even if in my living room, and the Hudson seemed more appropriate than the former.

After-work evening parlays had produced consistent catches of small stripers and snapper blues. Usually a dozen or more before dark, seldom larger than a couple of pounds, an occasional three-pounder. A sprinkling of shad and white perch. But tomorrow I would tempt and tease the trophy stripers that had so far eluded me. That had never even tasted one of my streamers.

I had just read Robert Boyle's *The Hudson River*. Not really a fishing book, but all the positive reinforcement I needed to believe in the 40-pounders. Montauk-size fish. They are there at 116th Street. I saw the pictures in the book. The first-hand accounts. The graphed soundings of the river bottom. Loaded with fish. Cow stripers, traveling upriver to winter-over at Storm King. Exhibiting deep-water feeding frenzies. Their mouths engulfing whole snappers and menhaden—and tomorrow: weighted, tinseled streamers.

The past two weeks had been hot and sticky, humid with not a drop of rain. Clouds building up slowly in advance of the low that would move through tomorrow evening. A low-pressure area, following days and days of sunshine. Fish time. Feeding time. And Robert Boyle's knowledge new and fresh to me. I was certain to fulfill my hopes.

I had changed my tackle. The eight-and-a-half-foot graphite rod now had, instead of the number-six floating line, a number-eight fast-sinking line. The 50 yards of 12-pound Dacron was now 150 of 20-pound. The size six and eight streamers were still in the bandaid can, but joining them were heavily weighted two's and three's. Thick with tinsel and marabou. Some black, some white, some both. I would fish deep—not the three to five feet I always had—but deep where Boyle's monsters are. Twenty, 30 feet and more. Out from the bank, *into* the river. Letting the fly search the shadows. Not merely skim the surface. I would fish new. I was ready, primed, built up.

The weather was perfect—in the past I had always caught more Hudson stripers preceding rainfall. And the tide—charts indicated a nine A.M. high. I would fish the last two hours of the incoming, and then the outgoing. Perfect. The only thing that could spoil the conditions would be a heavy sewage flow. There is no schedule for that.

My tackle was ready for a daybreak departure. I lay, unsuccessfully attempting sleep. The Hudson flowed in my brain. Its beginning at the Mt. Marcy–shadowed Lake Tear. The fishless two-acre Lake Tear of the Clouds. Spilling gently down, gradually becoming the wild, trout-rich upper Hudson. At the base of the mountains the river is cowed by locks and dams. The trout become carp. The clear, cold tributaries become sludgy, sudsy paper-mill outfalls. Troy adds its sewage. Once past the Troy Dam, the river first tastes salt. The tides reach up 154 miles, past Poughkeepsie, West Point, Croton, Haverstraw Bay, Spuyten Duyvil, the George Washington Bridge, 116th St. The ocean working its way up into Manhattan's sewer. The carp become stripers. The stripers that I have just read about. Seventeen million of them, says Boyle. Many of them well into heavy poundage. One of which I sleep on and tussle with throughout the night.

The pre–dawn alarm cut the battle short, and soon I was walking across Broadway towards Riverside Park. The sky dark before me and lighting behind. The park void of life. The riverside highway crammed with early-morning commuters. Through which I scurry to the river's edge.

My 116th Street beat. A rocky stretch of bank, extending two blocks to the concrete sewer outlet on my left, and eight blocks north to the slow bay south of 125th Street. Strewn with man-size rocks, not boulders, placed there as both highway support and river curb. Extending slowly to 30-foot depths along which stripers and baitfish cruise. Rocks laden with wood, rope, garbage, rats, debris of every kind. Rocks that shine with a green-black oily moss at low tide. Rocks that sometimes look even picturesque at the very highest tides. Tides that flood away the trash.

And today it was the latter. The tide still two hours from completion, the river was high and clean. Sewage flow could not be seen. Scattered snappers rose, disturbing the surface far out upon the flattened Hudson. Clouds were thick and low, and there was no wind. And the water erupted 50 feet out just as I had strung my rod.

A three-splash burst attracted the big streamer, and my first cast was upon a feeding striper. The line tightened as I began to strip it and then it stripped back at me. Short spurts of line left the single-action reel. The fish surfaced shallowly and I saw that it was a respectable striper. At least for me. For this beat. Another short run and the fish came in. Pulling solidly until I slid it onto the flat rock beneath me. A good striper, a little over three pounds. As large as I had taken here. Easing the hook from its lower jaw, I released him into the upstream current—following him into the surprising three-foot visibility of the river.

More casts brought more fish. All near the surface, all school fish of three pounds. My deep-water plans were being stymied by the frantic stripers. No matter where I cast, the fly was not allowed to drop into deep water. Parallel to the bank, even a double-hauled 70-footer was attacked. I thought of the previous year when the snappers had so treated me.

I had seen an advertisement for one of those inflatable canoes, large enough for three persons. The ad read, "Yours free, for 30 days." I ordered it, and Janet and I christened it on the Saturday that it arrived.

After eight minutes of foot-pumping, the canoe was ready, and Janet and I had clumsily clambered in and shoved off. The craft was surprisingly comfortable and the two-ended kayak paddle pushed it gently across the water.

Janet relaxed as I double-stroked us out towards mid-river. The breeze offered a watery mist as we encountered each small wave. I stopped paddling and the canoe settled into a comfortable drift. As did our thoughts.

We talked about spending future hot summer days out on the Hudson, I with a fly rod and Janet with a book and suntan lotion. We weren't considering returning the 150-dollar canoe in 30 days.

We lay back in either end of the canoe, my head on the stern, Janet's on the bow. Our eyes closed, we were in fantasy worlds—feeling the soft rocking of the waves and the heat of the sun. We dreamed of days to come on the river.

Janet dreamed a warm dream of togetherness. She and I paddling slowly past the George Washington Bridge, pausing for a loving kiss or a lazy conversation. Enjoying each other. Floating freely. Drinking homemade iced tea from a thermos. Lazy days.

I dreamed of big stripers. Of drifting live snappers and eels while simultaneously throwing streamers. I dreamed of schools of ravaging bluefish far away from the shore. Eight minutes with the foot pump and I would be among them. Janet would be welcome to come along. If she wanted.

Our dreams may have been interrupted by sleep except for the constant eye kept for approaching boats. We drifted, we paddled, we talked and laughed. I had long since fallen victim to the Hudson's charms, and it was finally charming Janet. She used words like "beautiful" and even "clean" to describe what she had previously called a cesspool.

Time avoided us and we noticed that we had drifted well upstream from our launching area. And that's when it happened. Sudden skittering snappers fleeing from resonant boilings in the surface summoned me to flex the waiting fly rod. Cast after cast, taking the ten-inch snappers, never connecting with the heavier feeder fish. The snappers all over my marabou fly, not allowing it to sink, not allowing it to be noticed by the big ones.

And so, it seemed, would be this cloudy autumn morning. With three-pound stripers substituting for the ten-inch snappers. There had to be a way to reach those deeper fish that I knew were there.

I twisted two strips of lead above my streamer, making it so heavy that it was difficult to cast. The first cast, near-missing my ear, splashed into the river and sank. It *sank*, quickly and deeply. I waited and watched and began to retrieve with a jerky hand-twist. Slowly, erratically, bumping along the bottom rocks, the fly bounced shoreward. Nothing. Not a strike. Another cast. And another. I removed the lead to see if the three-pounders were still there. They were. I replaced it and settled down to a long morning.

I threw the heavily weighted streamers farther and deeper, salmon-swinging them with the current. Tickling the river-bottom rocks. Hanging, and losing an occasional leader. I tried all of my big flies. The bulky ones, the sparse, the white, the black. Every so often reverting back to three-pound fish to test their presence.

High tide came and went. The river had been moving seaward for an hour when I got the first deep-water strike. Almost concurrent with the first tiny drop of rain. An unmistakable hit, I set the hook hard and reeled in a limp line. My leader, frayed from the rocks, had parted. I replaced it and tried again. Another strike, this time almost savage, and the rain began.

The graphite rod bent double and the reel's handle galloped wildly. Quickly into the backing, the fish set out towards New Jersey. Palming the reel, I broke the fish's speed, and it turned downriver. With the current. With me following. Jumping from rock to rock to rock. Surefootedly with a bending fly rod. And a backwards-turning reel. I dared not put too much pressure on the 12-pound leader.

I followed the fish for a long while, well past the southerly limit of my beat. Across never-before-stepped-upon rocks, past unfamiliar sewer outlets. Nearing the 96th Street underpass. The fish slowly taking line faster than I could follow. It was a big fish. Not the staccato jerks of the earlier schoolies, but a slow throbbing. I could visualize the massive jaws shaking and trying to dislodge the fly.

At 96th Street the fish slowed, and then stopped, turning to face the current. I gained a few feet of line, and then more as I cautiously pumped the three-ounce rod. The fish was tiring, and heading upstream, north. Very slowly. A couple of rocks per minute. A lot of time had passed and I was totally drenched now by the steady rain. And footing had become slippery. I stepped carefully as I retraced my path upriver.

Occasionally there were short runs, maybe 20 or 30 feet, no more. I was alone fighting a Hudson River cow striper, traffic speeding unnoticingly by, uncaring about the fish-fight of my life.

Thirty minutes, then an hour, the fish was still pulling, still deep into the backing. But *I* was winning now. A foot or two at a time—like you see in those marlin films. Only I was into a fly-rod striper. It *had* to be a big one. Not merely 20 or 30 pounds, but a whopper. I began to visualize the headlines, the outdoor magazines, the tackle-company endorsements. All the while the fish well outside my grasp.

Finally I saw the end of the fly line poke from the water. Then more and more. And then the first turn onto the reel. Only 90 more feet.

Nearer and nearer the fish came—now zigzagging up and downriver. Pulling strongly and tightly through the graphite and into my forearms. Straining the light cane-colored rod beyond its means. The line teasing the surface with Zorro lashes. Desperation.

At one point I slipped and my right leg went thigh-deep into the river. I lifted myself with one arm and felt a heavy rod in the other.

I planted myself onto a flat standing-rock, and readied myself for the finish. There was no place to beach the fish, so I would have to grab it by the jaw and hang on. My footing secure, I practiced kneeling to the water. It could be done—lipping the big striper.

The fish, mentally creeled now, made an unexpectedly strong surge. Not wanting to lose my vantage point, I palmed down hard on the reel and the line went flat. Limp. Dead. It was over. Gone, and I had never seen the fish. I breathed deeply with rain on my face that could have been tears. Just like that. I had made a mistake and the fish was gone. That was all.

The retrieved leader still had the streamer—bent and evidently torn from the fish's jaw. Only then did I notice the cold wind that was following the rain. Wind that signaled the passing of the weather. High skies and sunshine to follow.

Across traffic and into Riverside Park I watched the rain-soaked Saturday volleyballers taking down their nets. They played there every Saturday, and always eyed me with curiosity as I passed with my rod. As I did them. I guess we both wonder what the fun is in the other's sport.

The following weeks produced many more stripers, up to three pounds. Not a big one, though. But that's my beat, and I fish it often. Sewer and all. Although we seldom confine our angling to a single body or stretch of water, we do have certain brooks that feel most comfortable, special waters that have become a part of us, or we of them, and one particular beat where our sloppiest of hats can be hung with ease.

Gordon's Neversink, Schwiebert's Ausable, Bergman's Firehole, Marinaro's Letort, Lyons' "Left Branch of the Croydon," and *my* 116th Street Hudson.

*A shapely, handsome warrior worthy of anybody's rod.*

—LYNN BOGUE HUNT,
"Striped Bass and Ol' Devil Sea,"
in *Field and Stream,* March 1936

# 16

# The Joys of Fishing

### Emmett Gowen

T here are a blessed few who catch a striped bass on their first attempt, or even their first cast. Others achieve proficiency quickly through apprenticeship. However, for the majority of anglers, becoming skilled at striper fishing is a slow learning process, but one not without its rewards, as even small successes often carry much significance. Emmett Gowen, in The Joys of Fishing (1961), provides an evocative diary of his accidental discovery of striper fishing and his slow but eventual accomplishment through raw perseverance.

---

More people have fun fishing from bridges, jetties, and piers than from all the skiffs in the bays and all the cruisers and party boats beyond the tide line. The reason: it's good, sociable fishing. No large inventory of capital equipment is required; even the novice may yank a mess of fish out of the briny on a handline.

I will always love pier fishing, for itself and because it bridged the gap between sweet-water experience and broad ocean adventures. Variety is the spice of pier fishing, variety of fish and fishermen. The human comedy moves out from the cities onto the end of the pier and there, entangled with fish, becomes gently and beneficently hi-larious.

There was that day a writer named William Saroyan was break-ing himself in as an angler on a pier in the vicinity of Santa Monica. He rented a rod and reel. He baited up with one of those dried and salted anchovies which were standard bait there. An extremely per-ceptive man, Bill saw at once the basic principle of casting a bait from a pier. He hauled off and cast the hat of a man fishing beside him far out into the blue. The hat remained on the hook, and Bill fought and landed it. The man put his hat back on and went to fishing again. He practically thanked Bill. Said the hat was cooler anyway, now it was wet. Besides, it wasn't anything but a twenty-dollar Stetson. Bill got set again, hauled off and heaved another cast, and this time cast the same hat, off the head of the same man, just about twice as far. The repetition of the phenomenon was what rattled them both. Also the sinker had this time conked the man, which may have had some bearing on his loss of aplomb.

"Listen, you wop so-and-so!" cried the man.

"No, no," Bill said, offering his hand. "I'm an Armenian so-and-so."

The rest of the day the two hung over the railing together talking, refreshing themselves with beverages now and then.

See what I mean? Bill was undoubtedly getting literary material. Friends are made pier fishing. It would be safe to assume that even romances are begun there, telephone numbers acquired, perhaps even blondes picked up. Pier fishing is for the sociable and anything can happen.

Also, it is for catching eating fish. Pier fishermen, fisherwomen, and fisherchildren, as a class, don't care about the rules of angling, about catching the biggest fish on the smallest tackle, and rarefying the sport to the point of throwing the fish back. They fish to get the fish, for dietary purposes. On this low-brow plane the sport is as good as the best, and a little better.

On that same Santa Monica pier one sunset I was present when a school of mackerel came by. People were using long cane poles, with mackerel jigs. I rented me one, I forget how much, maybe two bits. Swinging out the jig, I'd set it moving and the strike would bend the pole double. Then, with the springy pole, I'd fight the mackerel in swift circles. I would get it to the surface. As soon as it lost its traction, its weight was less than my pull and here would come a fine wet mackerel aimed at my face. I would dodge numbly and sack up another one. All the other folks there were doing the same thing—men whooping and hollering and shouting advice and one thing or another, women screaming with thrill and delight, children darting excitedly amongst adult legs, and the freshly landed mackerel slapping the pier planking.

A score of us at this fishing, with these interlocking and entangling crises, made a wild scene of sport and excited fun. The hazard was being smacked with a wet mackerel, but who cared. All were atavistically taking subsistence from the primitive depths, wild fish from the undomesticated ocean. Life was timeless and wonderful, and when the school of mackerel moved out of reach most of us hefted each his sackful and plodded in the dusk from outdoors adventure to the glitter and glory of Los Angeles, a few yards away.

As an angler progresses from the starting point of his career as a pier fisherman, he might get to want to catch a particular species of fish. In the beginning of pier fishing you drop a baited hook to see what you will pull up. With time and experience this becomes foretellable. For example, at a certain stage of my own pier-fishing career, I wanted to catch an oceanic striped bass.

I kept trying for this angling adventure from the sea wall of the inlet at Point Lookout, Long Island. What a fishing spot this was! I would bait with sandworms or bloodworms and catch weakfish, porgies, or croakers. Killies would get fluke. But a large skimmer clam was the best. This would catch anything, including big blackfish. One summer Sunday I was sitting there happily fishing, using my method of that period of my angling history. The rocks were crowded with us subway fishing-trippers, and others were using methods no more classy than mine. For instance, one rig popular with Italians, it seemed, was a handline attached to a jingle bell on a spring, the bell on one end, the other end sharpened. They would cast the handline, stick the bell up in the pier planking, and lie back in the sun or get a drink of red wine out of the lunch basket containing the pastrami and cold pizza pie, and wait for the bell to ring. It was a charming way to fish.

My own method came of my Southern angling heritage. I liked to go fishing with an armful of rods and reels. I would bait and throw out a rig; getting another rig out gives something to do while waiting for a bite on the first one. I inherited my first fishing tackle from a great uncle. Uncle Jeff was a rodmaker of ability and there were a dozen beautiful bamboo rods to use with the old-time Kentucky-made reels. Every one of these rods had a copper fluke on the butt, sharpened for sticking into the mud of a stream bank.

That day at Point Lookout I had three rod sets. There was one reel that had some teeth missing from its cogs, I reckon: you never heard so small an object as a fishing reel make such a racket as that defective one.

I had the rod butt set in a crack between the big jetty rocks, and all was tranquil; the tide just getting slack, low, which ought to improve the fishing. Suddenly this reel began to give its loud metallic scream, something like a motor racing on dry bearings. I dashed and grabbed up the rod, gasping with the excitement of a strike. When I felt what I had on there, I knew a big moment had come; what it was I knew not, but this big fish was going down the tide and even reckless pressure upon the throbbing rod slowed it not a bit. It was big, really big, at that time of my oceanic fishing experience.

The instantaneous action which was indicated was to run like a mountain goat over the rocks of the jetty, to go down the tide with my fish. I stepped between lovers sunning themselves on the rocks, ran across a family picnic spread, stumbled over one person's lap and fell into another's. But stay with my fish I must, and while my line swept up all the lines which were not hauled in out of its way, I ran over anybody in my path. (It was all taken as good fun, or so I recall.) I stepped in somebody's lunch pie—oh, that was all right; I was a man with a big fish, and the owner of the pie also wanted badly to see it caught.

Finally at the end of the rocks, where the beach began, the fish ran out of gismo and began to turn. I worked it gradually in close and then I saw it. A striper! What a graceful silver fish, brightness set off by dark horizontal streaks.

Four or five young fellows jumped into the water to help me land it. I was afraid somebody would take hold of the line and give the fish a chance by a sudden lurch to break off, so I was bawling, "Grab the fish, not the line." Finally our collective effort wrestled it onto the sand—thirteen pounds of bass, a very gratifying catch. That successful fishing trip cost me subway fare to the end of the line, bus fare of ten cents on out to the point, and maybe two bits for a dozen clams.

It had taken nothing more than a clam to involve me in the excitement and thrill of striped-bass fishing. That was during the wartime years when I was fishing for whatever would bite. A thirteen-pound striped bass took the clam, and that striped bass caught me. My fishing diary, a record of hope and frustration during this period of concentrated pursuit of the species, began late in the fall. Large omissions from this epic journal were caused either by having less than nothing to write, or by having wage-earning labor to do. . . .

NOVEMBER 20    "Now that I've caught a striped bass on bait, it's the big league for me. Artificials. A tin squid or plug, and a fine long cast, then a big striper. To a hillbilly bait fisherman, this "block tin squid" looks no more than a shiny, tapered sinker and am for hanging something edible on the hooks. But will refrain, having made stern self-promise to follow rigid code. I aim to use big wooden or plastic "plugs" too, that have three gang hooks; they will hold a lot of worms, I can tell, but will resist."

NOVEMBER 21    "Fished Shinnecock Inlet. Cold. Northeast winds shifting to north. The N.E. winds spoiled casting by blowing a bow in line, looping the slack over reel handle. Several surf fishermen were there waiting in their cars with a certain thoughtful and knowing expression, characteristic of fishing experts. Motor dory out there trolling, taking stripers out in the middle of the inlet. Dangerous?

"At sunset the casters waded out. Low tide just at dark, an ideal striper situation, I think. Apparently a school came in and sped past, leaving one fish each for most of the 'squidders' [those who use block-tin-squid casting tackle with tin squids or other heavy jig] who stood there in a row, fighting fish. None for me. I have a feeling of being used unfairly. I watch the experts and imitate them."

NOVEMBER 22    "An old man fishing in the surf with worms. 'Worms?" I asked eagerly. 'Yes, real late, when the fishing is nearly over, they bite on worms here.' It was very cold. Needed gloves standing still fishing. He told me this:

" 'Once, in a southeast storm, on the east side of the inlet, I was alone. The fish were hitting as fast as I could cast. The Coast Guardsman in the tower was watching with a glass, and he told them on this side, "There's a fellow over there catching fish as long as he is." They all jumped into their cars and came ten miles around. A boy with a short boat rod caught a twenty-pounder so close in that the fish ran into my legs and knocked me down. If you made a long cast you got the little ones. The big ones were inside the breakers.'

"In the afternoon, as the tide went out, the gulls became busy over the bar at the inlet. I thought they must be after baitfish, which also draw stripers, and I got excited: 'The gulls are working!' I remarked, hurrying off toward the spot.

" 'They're not working over bass,' the old man called. I stopped.

" 'How do you tell?'

" 'They're feeding on a kind of worm that goes into the bay to spawn, and then leaves.' This was so, I saw them. The worms were a foot long, segmented like tapeworms, drifting out on the tide, the gulls snatching them out of the water.

"Tonight's bitter N.W. cold wind ends a striper season. Not a fish all season."

JUNE 15  "Well, maybe this second year will be better. East side of Shinnecock Inlet. Chilly and rainy. The regular striper followers—a couple in the station wagon equipped for sleeping, a fellow who wears yachting cap, also a redheaded expert—all caught fish. Resolution wavered. Ashamed to fish with bait before these squidders, so I drove to the other side of the inlet. Squidded futilely awhile, then rigged and baited with some dead sandworms left in the car from a previous weakfish trip.

"I caught a twelve-pound striper, but on bait. Consolation, but not success; squidding is what I am trying to solve, not bait fishing. The fellow the other experts call Red came along right behind where I had been squidding, made a cast, took a blue bigger than ten pounds, and went back to his car, just like that. He was too scornful of a novice even to glance my way, although we two and the dying fish were the only creatures in a vast desert solitude of sea and sand."

JULY 2   "Shinnecock Inlet again. Stripers at high tide breaking water way out on the outer bar. This put me out of my mind. I considered making a raft of driftwood to fish from, but reconsidered—a wave would pitch me off and then use my raft to bash in my head. There they were, a big school of them just out of reach. At low tide I could finally get there, water waist-deep and waves to my neck, but then the stripers were gone.

"Defeated, I went down under the light tower and watched the harpooners bring swordfish through the inlet. Nine giant fish were brought past the point, some boats with one, some two or more. One fisherman, commercial, put in at the Coast Guard slip. He and the crew—two men and a boy—had caught eight hundred pounds. He was a tall, thin man, burned nearly black, in dungarees and surf cap. His sea skiff was a beauty, clean and white, with motor of great h.p. for its size.

"He had cleverly rigged the fish, rolled in rope so that when he handed the line to volunteers up on the dock all they had to do was pull collectively to roll the fish into the boat. He bantered with a woman about whether she wanted to can a tuna he had, this fish about six hundred pounds. I noticed two other smaller fish in the boat. Going from stowing his big fish, quick and agile, he kissed his fingertips and touched them to the big fish.

"From the sociable remarks, his story of the catch emerged. 'There were fifteen of them,' he said. 'Got him up this far out of the water, and we had to stop up the scuppers. I decided to let him hang out. It was tedious coming in, with that drag.'

"One of the crew said, 'I didn't know which one he wanted me to get. Struck right down in the middle of them. Just luck it was the big one.' "

SEPTEMBER 9   "Took the editor of my novel surf fishing with the idea of entertaining him. Gave him my best rod and reel. The occasion was not a fishing success. The trawlers and draggers have dragged the waters clean of fish, I think. It seems impossible to catch a fish from the surf. In the second place, I have only one fishing suit, so we fished in swimming trunks. It was cold. I showed him how to cast. He was confident, being an expert fresh-water caster. He made a few frustrated tries. Then he put everything into it, and succeeded in flinging himself violently down in the surf. Tried not to laugh. I'm afraid my novel got its hind end doused in cold water too, right there.

"I told him it takes a couple of years to learn to cast a big surf rod. Told him how, my first year of surf fishing, I would have my wife hold the rod and reel while I swam out with the hook and sinker and dropped it, that satisfying my determination to get far enough out to catch fish. We had caught them, too—weaks, fluke, croaker—but it was an exhausting method.

"If one is to be a surf fisherman I believe it is necessary to buy tackle and go out on the beach and begin struggling against frustration. In a season you can learn to make short casts. It will be about the third season, when you have tackle more nearly correct, and have learned to balance it up as to rod, reel, line, weight of sinker, etc., that you find it an easy-looking flip of the arms to send your rig sailing away out beyond the bar."

SEPTEMBER 22   "Tried for stripers at Shinnecock Inlet, Montauk Point, Montauk Beach. Caught nothing but a few blowfish, a skate and a fluke, all on shedder crabs. No other fisherman admitted catching anything. The familiar dory, however, was trolling dangerously in Shinnecock Inlet and taking them. Last Monday, in a northeast gale, the stripers were biting famously, everywhere."

NOVEMBER 6   "Last Saturday, November 3, we set out for Shinnecock Inlet. Were told at Altenkirk's tackle store that they had not been striking at the inlet, but had been at Montauk Point. So we went on. A dozen or so people fishing the point, but they were not catching any. I went around to Mr. Clark's, the fishing shack in the north cove. Mr. Clark and his helper were just lifting the pound net. Mostly stripers, 'two boxes' of them, some cod, some weakfish, and a sturgeon. This was a poor day's catch, Mr. Clark said. The fishing was falling off. Earlier they had been getting a boatful.

"Just before dark three fellows came down to the spot known as Jones', one of them the redheaded and unsociable expert. They had on waders and went out up to their chests on the reef, began casting, and right away caught fish. Then a man not casting so far caught one. I, next in line, got none. Well, now I have part of it. That spot, far out, could be reached with waders. Boots and a rubberized suit had limitations.

"Went back to Shinnecock to try there in the dawn. Turned cold and began to rain in the night. Fished in the dawn with my hands freezing, but got nothing. Saw two fish break, and cast to the spot but with no luck. Then back to Montauk. It was raining hard all day, and cold. People were fishing on the idea that it was striper weather—violent.

"One fellow had fallen down in the surf and was soaking wet. He had a fire, and a piece of tin jutting from the side of the bluff to keep the rain off his head, trying to dry. I tried to dry my clothes, but they would get wet on one side while the other was drying. He saw a fish break a time or two and started fishing then, soaking wet in that cold! I gave up. Went back to Hampton Bays to try Shinnecock again in the dawn. Again, no luck."

NOVEMBER 10   "Claire and I at Jones' Inlet. Rainy, overcast, north wind. A number of fishermen here, but only one fellow caught fish, first one and then a second, as though a school had come in close and left soon. He had a bright lure, no feather in it. Ah-ha—the secret is the lure! No feathers."

NOVEMBER 15   "Shinnecock Inlet. Poured all day. People fishing with worms, like the old man had said last November. Some big ones had been caught here recently to forty pounds. Three had been caught by the valiant dory man trolling in the inlet the night before. The dory belongs to a Coast Guard officer. He and a young A.B. fish in it when off duty.

"Dreary and boring fishing in the rain. Got annoyed with Claire for walking our setter Red Bar in the pour, although her pastime while I fish is to walk while the setter romps over the dunes. In anticipation [correct, too] that tomorrow will be very cold, we are going to drive home. Our fishing success has been poor this past season.

"It seems to me that it would be a magnificent experience, hauling a fine big striper out of the cold water in these days of gloomy sky, wind, roaring breakers, and rain, but that experience has been denied me. I have now flung a tin squid for two years, without ever catching a fish on one. Nothing works. I believe stripers make quick and brief excursions along the surf and then are gone, for hours or perhaps days, and you have to be there at just the moment. Maybe it's the right moment that I am missing."

November 22   "Shinnecock again. There is a terrible rip here, as all the great bay must pour in and out across a narrow and shallow inlet. In this swam a goose some hunter had winged, and into this Red Bar's Irish-setter instincts impelled him on a literal wild-goose chase. The rip caught him and was swiftly taking him toward sure death in the breakers. Claire ran along the dunes screaming, trying to call him back. I didn't see it.

"The Coast Guardsmen invited Claire aboard and put out in the crashboat. They pulled Red Bar aboard just short of the deadly surf. 'It's a good thing he didn't catch that goose,' the Coast Guardsman told Claire. 'It would have whipped him and pecked his eyes out.' Red Bar shook water all over them and made to jump back after the goose."

September 4   "My third year. Thought maybe this would be the one! Tuesday, Claire and I set out on a three-day fishing trip. Fished afternoon, evening, and next dawn at Narraganset rocks, west of Narraganset Pier in Rhode Island. Not a touch. Heard fishing had been good there in August. Jerry Sylvester, tackle store, said they were there, but were big and smart. A famous expert of the Atlantic Coast, he recommended a blue plug of his own design. I, with pre-conceptions, bought three small eels as rigged by him at 50 cents apiece. Hard to cast an eel downwind, and impossible against the wind. So I used a tin squid mainly, anyhow.

"Next day Claire and I drove on to Cape Cod Canal. Here the story was that good fishing had been in July. Thought of hunting for stripers on Martha's Vineyard, but there was so much futility that I was oppressed by the idea. What a silly pursuit, for a man who must also pursue earning a living. At home the newspapers were piled up at the door, and I read in the rod-and-gun columns that the stripers were biting fine. Especially at Martha's Vineyard! This is my third year of unbroken, total failure to get one squidding. I am through."

September 9   "People fishing in Shinnecock Inlet, nobody catching anything except the Coast Guard pair, who troll four short handlines, two on stubby outriggers, two over the stern. The surf-fishing set are out, however, sitting in their cars, waiting. They are for me the best signs of fish. The bluefish came in last night and are being caught over the bar where the water is no more than a foot deep. For something to do, I caught a fluke on a piece of squid.

"An hour before dark the most eager of the surf hounds were out—merely to pick the place they consider best, I believe. The most eager of all, the young man the others call Red, went farthest out into the point, withstood more buffeting by waves, cast farther, etc. He caught the first fish, too; just before dark, just after the tide changed.

"Later I walked down the beach, casting into the moon path diffidently, enjoying being there, not really hoping to catch a fish, but wishing of course for the great and seemingly impossible luck—dreaming of it, rather."

SEPTEMBER 20  "Point Lookout. Upon arrival saw line of surf casters way out. Just sunset. All were wrestling with fish—small blues and large weaks. I went out as far as I could in boots. Not far enough. Went back and took off the boots and also my pants and went out again. First cast, a strike! A blue. Another cast, a weak. Then lost two and got worried about my pants and Red Bar there in the dark for a thief to come along and find. Tied my stuff around my neck, to carry it out with me. Red Bar, deprived of his home base on the beach, left shore with me and remained swimming around behind me. It occurred to me then that three times I have missed fish for lack of waders. At least now I have finally caught a fish on an artificial, even if it was not a striper."

OCTOBER 14  "Montauk Point. Warming weather after a northeast wind of several days, which has changed to east. When we got here, there were glistening stripers laid out on the beach. They were in! I got to work fervently, but could not get beyond the heave. A few more fish were caught on long casts after I got there. Red caught them. I merely lost tin jigs on account of the rough water wrapping the long casts around rocks. Rule one: At Montauk, if you get a backlash, wind it right on in and make a cast on the beach to get the backlash out, otherwise you lose your lure.

"Slept in the car. Woke at 3:00 A.M., or rather was awakened by a man whose car was parked nearby, grumbling to his companions about fish hogs. 'They're killing them, but there are two or three fellows who wade out in front of you so you can't cast,' he said. This would be Red. I'll go try, I thought.

" 'It's just about over now,' he added.

"I decided to sleep a little more. But couldn't sleep, and finally went down. The 'fish hog' was just coming out—Red, with a string of six stripers all above ten pounds. Two or three others were leaving with fish. Well, I had missed them, that time, but I had been close to both place and moment.

"Strikes me that when the stripers come in, even though it be 3:00 A.M. far out at the end of Montauk Point, even in a storm, there are too many fishermen, so that some have complaints about being crowded from the spot where the fish are. But Red, for all my envy, is plainly a real sportsman. Envy called him 'fish hog.' He doesn't crowd anybody. He just strolls past the aspirants, goes on out to start casting about where we leave off. Often he lets his waders fill to hold him down, no matter how cold the water.

"And he uncannily lays a cast right into the open face of a striper, often first lick. He takes a few quickly, and with such regal arrogance that even cold salt water can't make him shiver. The striper experts are all unsociable, unlike the general run of fishermen. But when you drive up to a fishing spot and see them, you know the stripers are coming in. They don't work all the time fishing. They go down just at whatever tide the fish are coming in on, catch some, and then rest in their cars, casual, idle, and exclusive."

OCTOBER 16   "The stripers struck on Jones' Reef, so I got an early start to have my place on that reef and not give it up to anybody. The blues did come in at sunset. They caught them on both sides of me. They came in and broke fifteen feet in front of me, in two feet of water. Not a one touched my lure. I cursed the lures, then. Backlashes, broken lines, knots in the lines. Ran out of line and lures and dashed back to Montauk to get more, but got the wrong kind of lure and a terrible piece of some kind of cheap and no-good line. Bad luck, bad luck. Then come to find out, right around the corner of the bluff the stripers had been in at sunset; some caught three or four. Forty or more were taken. And I had not known about it!

"Next time, don't work so hard, but look for signs of fish. The couple who go in a station wagon named 'The Beachcombers' do this, with glasses. I bought a ten-pound striper for $3.50.

"During the day I forswore fishing for stripers, having worked for them all summer with never a one. But an old Italian lucked up a stray twenty-four-pounder on a short and inept cast! With small eels for bait. Generously he gave me two.

" 'But they are spoiled; they stink,' I said.

" 'Feesh-ah no pa'ticula',' he said."

OCTOBER 18 "Got to thinking: Now I knew just how to do it. Hurried back to Montauk before weather, moon, and tide changed and put this knowledge in effect. First, while Claire prepared two days' food, I went into the city and shopped for just the kind of lures I wanted. I had never tried a nylon line but bought one because I had heard it could be cast farther. But I was doubtful of this, so also bought a new linen line.

"Got started in the afternoon and drove just above the speed limit, to be there for the sundown fishing. On the way bawled Claire out for the things we had forgotten in haste. Reflected: the magic mood of country catfishing, the calmness, has worn off this hillbilly. What has done it? I am a hurried and harried New Yorker, even in fishing and despite an old determination to never lose my calm.

"Got here just at sundown. The nylon line seemed wonderful—way, way out beyond the heave the lure would go. Made about six of these casts, much longer than ever before—magnificent, twice as long. Then the lure touched a rock, and I struck with my rod to bounce it over, and the line snapped in two.

"Put on a new tin squid, tried again, and got a backlash. Reeled in quickly and cast to the beach to get the backlash out. This dry-land cast did not quite expose the bird's nest, so I pulled off the remaining few feet, and damned if the line didn't fall in two of its own accord this time. Tied it up and cast again. Touched a rock and struck, and the line went in two a third time. Went to the car, muttering that I had been swindled, that the off-brand line was completely no good, and at the same time congratulating myself of the luck that had made me have a linen line on the extra Penn Squidder reel.

"Put this on, and was back at the gulls working over the fish got closer and closer to the point. Found a good place where I had seen fish caught before, and said to myself, 'I've got the right lure, am in the right spot and a little farther out than all except one. If any fish are caught, I will be in on it.'

"But I wasn't. Another man got one; the only fish caught. He turned to wade in and I saw into his parka hood—Red! Fished a couple more hours to get good and tired and be sure I could sleep at once. I'm getting up for the low tide, high moon, at 3:00 A.M. This fact is the secret of it all, I am sure."

OCTOBER 19  "Awoke at the right time and waded out on the reef. A man there was just taking one off a plug. Two or three were caught on plugs. My plug was up in the car, and the fish would be gone by the time I could get it. So I worked my tin jig a little, and got nothing, while several more were brought in on plugs. Now I knew a little more; be down there the next morning, high moon and low tide, with a plug. After that, I squidded all day, back and forth along the beach, practically wearing out a line but conserving it enough for the strategy of getting the fish tomorrow on a plug. Claire cooked dinner on a campfire—beans and coffee. Ate in the sunset and high wind and this was pleasant.

"Chose the same spot for the sundown fishing. The fish broke almost close enough, and you could see the gulls working over another school, closer and closer. But the boats kept trolling back and forth between the fish and the beach, gunning their motors and herding the fish out. Banking on my new theory, I will sleep tonight balled up in the car."

OCTOBER 20  "Woke at what I guessed to be the right time, but decided to rest one more moment. Next time I woke there was light in the east. Too late! Went down with my plug, however. There lay fish on the beach; four or five men still out up to their armpits on the reef. One of them was the ineffable and unsociable Red. But they're too hard to get. It doesn't pay. No more striper fishing for me.

"Stopped at Shinnecock on the way home to give Red Bar his run, before returning to the city. South wind was roughing the water and two or three gulls were working close in. As I got to the spot the gulls abandoned it. Cast and cast, but raised nothing. Did see a blue break. It was just low tide. A gull worked out in the outer bar a while and then went away.

"The tide had started in. Just a moment too late here, too. Apparently they come in more on the outgoing tide, and just at low tide; apparently best when this is just before daybreak.

"On the way home bought a small tuna (nine pounds), three

pecks of oysters, and a couple of pecks of clams. Also about a dozen smoked eels. We opened the windows, had two or three drinks, fifteen oysters and a piece of steak. Cleaned my tackle a little and went to bed in the middle of the afternoon."

OCTOBER 21   "Awoke about 11 o'clock this morning. Claire and Red Bar slept that way, too. Got up aching a little from the strenuous fishing. But felt good, and purged of everything that had been worrying or bothering me. That is what a fishing trip does for me, whether I catch fish or not."

OCTOBER 25   "Got new braided-nylon line. Am confident I have precisely the right tackle, and prepared for Montauk Point again."

OCTOBER 26   "Had an idea on what tide the fish would come in. Got here 12:30, or 1:30, or God knows exactly what time. Went down to Jones'. Made two or three casts to get the line wet. Then a fine cast, way out just this side of the breakers on the reef, just *beyond* the white water.

"Instantly I felt a fish! Then I calmly and correctly landed the first striped bass I ever caught on a tin jig. I waded in with him and let the waves lift him out onto the rocks where he was secure. Rushed back, cast, felt a strike, and began bringing in another fish. Lord!

"In excitement I fooled with the star drag. As a matter of fact I released the drag altogether, and played the fish with my thumb, a small one, about four pounds. I gaffed it with my fingers, lifted it up under my left arm, removed the hook, and strung it.

"Cast again, and hooked one. Ah, I thought, pretty good size. Then I realized that it was a big one! I began fumbling in a messy combination of star drag and release of drag and using the thumb. The procedure worked all right as long as I could give full attention to it. It failed because, backing out of the surf, I became entangled in my previous two fish on the long stringer. I held the fish with both drag and thumb, with the mistaken idea of leaning the rod forward for the next surge while I untangled my feet. Now there was a loud pop above my head, startling and for an instant mystifying because I had never before heard forty-five-pound-test nylon break under strain.

"I had got into them at last. How delicious those bass were, broiled."

NOVEMBER 1    "Shinnecock Inlet. Stripers hitting on the out-going. Southeast storm, with big seas rolling. The line of regulars were working them from the shore of the inlet. Coast Guard officer's dory bobbling on the waves, taking fish. Wind rammed itself down our throats, and people walked at odd tilts, leaning into it, making glowing silhouettes in the eerie storm light.

"Somebody saw a wave crest break over the dory and drown the engine. At once the pair of seamen fishing from the dory did the cor-rect thing—they threw the anchor out. We surf casters stopped to watch. It remained difficult to admit real and immediate fear for them, although the danger was very obvious.

"Both figures in the boat worked over the engine. One jerked the starter rope, then the other impatiently tore it out of his hands and tried it himself.

"Their faces turned toward the Coast Guard tower. You could tell the officer was yelling something, but the wind blew his words away and his open mouth was soundless. Both donned life preservers.

"Now we realized the rip was so strong the dory was dragging anchor. Two men climbed down from the tower in frantic haste. They ran to the sheltered slip and in a moment rounded the inside point in the Coast Guard crashboat, out into the rip.

"We thought they were only going to make it four drownings in-stead of two, which now seemed certain. A breaker crashed over the dory. Then it was there again, full of water, both men still in it cling-ing to its gunwales. By expert seamanship and timing, the coxswain brought the crashboat through the surf and the second sailor, man-ning lines and life rings, threw two rings into the dory, out of which big fish were washing. A wave yanked the two boats apart and the men in the dory, knowing the life rings as the last chance for life, saw them jerked away. They jumped after them—and missed.

"The dory sank, beaten under. The two men made separate and differing decisions. The youth had the seamanship and the nerve to swim in the direction opposite to what his instinct must surely have urged him. He went with the rip, swimming out to sea.

"The other one had only twenty feet or so to reach the outer bar, which probably he could even see in the trough behind a crest, barely submerged from where he was. He made it and stood on it.

"One moment he stood only waist deep; then a torrent would break down upon him and knock him down. When it would pass, there he would be standing again. Many, many times this happened, but it couldn't go on too long. He couldn't see the boat behind him, for the breakers. But we all knew if it came to him it would be smashed at once on the bar. Apparently, however, he knew some maneuver by which they could reach him, for he kept yelling in the direction of the Coast Guard tower, making perfectly incomprehensible signals and then shaking his fist in rage because there wasn't a thing anybody could understand to do. He could have waded ashore along the bar but for the speed of that rip. I think he must have wanted the tower men, who could see the crashboat, to signal it to quit what it was doing and come after him. Men tried to yell to him to do as the sailor had done; swim and ride the rip on through the surf to the outside. He raged, shaking his fist.

"The crashboat went on through the surf and waited. Soon the other young seaman, the one adrift, came on through, fighting waves but carried by the rip. Here in water rough but not sure death like the surf, they pulled him aboard. And then the boat came in, riding high in a breaker just behind the crest, until the crest broke and it came on then sliding like a surf board. It looked for an instant as if, stern up-ended, it would dive into the shallow bottom, but the bow came up. Nobody ever witnessed cleaner and cooler fearlessness and skill than that of the Coast Guard coxswain.

"His officer was still standing on the bar, but now he was not cursing or gesticulating. When a wave would cover him, and then when he emerged again, he seemed confused, blinded, lost as to direction and perhaps hope, finally.

"Then I saw Red. I was astounded, and I cursed him. Red was fishing, calmly throwing a preliminary line-wetting cast.

"Then he threw a beauty, leaning forward in pause and stance and follow-through, his red-freckled face upraised to watch the high-soaring lure. It sailed right over and a few feet beyond the man on the bar. He could have caught the line, as Red intended he should, but he seemed not to notice.

"I still didn't understand, until a man whom Red had instructed began lining us up with our surf rods.

" 'When he catches Red's line, then the rest of us will tie our lines on. Cut your rigs and be ready.' We understood, then. Six or seven nine-thread lines together, pulled out to the man, would be strong as rope.

"But when the wave flattened out and the man should have been there again, he simply was not there. Red reeled in so fast his hand was a blur, not forgetting, however, to level-wind the line back and forth across his reel with the thumb of the hand forward of the rod butt. He took a stance ready to cast again—waiting.

"The man was gone. There was no need for Red to keep standing there, his appearance exactly like a surf caster watching for fish to break. No need at all . . ." [The body was never recovered.]

NOVEMBER 17 "Estimated low at Montauk Point would be around 11:00 A.M. and that is the tide they were coming in on now. I got here in time, but was told they had come in on the high the night before. I had made the trip, so I fished the rest of the day. I was ready to give up in despair after just one more cast with a plug in the dark. Made the try and was backing out of the surf, drawing in the plug and got a strike, but missed. Began casting some more.

"A strike! A fish! He came in without much struggle. About eight pounds. Went to the car, repaired a line, ate some sandwiches, fixed the car seat for sleeping, put Red Bar inside a tool shack there for the night, which was cloudy and looked like rain, and went back.

"Tide going out strong, now. Other fishermen began arriving, talking happily about the fishing of the night before. I kept my place, the farthest out. Comment: 'They'll have to make this place bigger.' Red, whom for three years now I have seen at the striper spots with never a word spoken between us, was there. He was the first to get a strike. Said it did not feel like a striper. It just pulled. 'Must be an angler,' someone commented. He hauled in by main force.

"Just as he got it to him the fish made its final break for freedom and broke the line, and then Red hollered it had been a damn big striper. Red tied on another plug, and in a moment had another strike. Then he thought he had a fish, but couldn't budge anything. Finally his line came in, empty. He said he had had a fish; I think his line might have been hung. A nylon line can fool you that way, it stretches so and throbs in waves.

"Then somebody caught one. Others got strikes. Red was a little behind in the running. A fellow next to me got a strike, slipped and fell. Unable to get up in the wash without using his hands which were winding frantically, and with just his head above water, he cried, 'Lift me up!' I went to do this for him, but then he realized the fish was gone and so he could take time to get up himself. I repressed an impulse to complain aloud that everyone was getting strikes but me. Just then I got one—a hard one. The line began running out in hard, big jerks. 'Don't cast over me, I've got a big one,' I cried.

"They waited. It was courteously decided that I might pass along the line of fishermen to get on the down-tide side, so they could resume fishing. 'He's a big one!' I kept saying. He kept going out. I hadn't brought him in a bit. I was careful this time, resolved to let the bass run in any case whatever, to redeem my having broken the line on that other big fish.

"At last I began retrieving line. It was dark, and I thought the fish was still pretty far out, when to my surprise it broke right close to me. I carried it out on a wave and dragged it up the beach. Not so big as I thought, but a fat sow; eighteen pounds, I would say. Went back out and began casting again. Meanwhile Red got more strikes and did not catch any. He went to help his friend gaff a fish and then came back and complained about his lack of space.

"Using his tactic, my armpit high waders sipping ice water, I moved farther out and away from him, but somebody else came in close to him on the other side. I couldn't see him very well, but I could feel his outrage. 'What, somebody out farther than I?' But I did not feel guilty for being taller than he.

" 'It's too crowded here for me!' Red said bitterly, and quit fishing in a huff.

" 'Come back, Red, you're among friends,' someone said humiliatingly. Red went on in and did not come back.

"Immediately I caught another fish, distracted from the thrill, however, by thinking of Red and by the worried emotions the long-odds horse must have when he comes abreast the favorite. The fish made a great surging run and immediately four people cast their plugs across my line. The man next to me quit fishing and went into service to systematically detach the plugs as my retrieving of line brought them in. This striper weighed eight pounds.

"Another cast, another fish—and a good one. This one I fought calmly, even nonchalantly, assured at last. I strung him, deciding these were enough for the night."

I had it now. I could take all of those hard-learned scraps of knowledge, of wind, tide, moon, season, baitfish, fish signs, and make an estimate of when and where, and sometimes be right. Never mind cold water in my waders, or a wave dashing into my face, or even risk of drowning. Never mind anything but the impassioned pursuit of the fish. This is what it's like to be a striper fisherman.

*Each of us who chases striped bass has some particular place that above all others sums up the essence of the endeavor. I love to catch them in the pounding surf, particularly in daylight when I can see the swirl of a great tail as the fish hits a surface plug, or when the sun is low and I can see their dark, heavy shapes hanging in the glassy green of a big wave whose top is about to tumble.*

—NELSON BRYANT,
*Memories of Striped Bass,* in *Fishing the East Coast,*
*Outdoor Life Guide,* 1980

# 17

# On Urban Shores

*Jan Frazier*

S|triper fishing on the gritty waterfront of New York Harbor offers an ambiance that is unique in the fishing world. Hot spots include rotting piers and sewer outfalls. The urban fisherman is a lonely pioneer in a city of millions, more likely to meet the underworld and vermin than a fellow angler. Ian Frazier's On Urban Shores (1994), is an offbeat look at the challenges and rewards of chasing stripers along the banks of Manhattan and the outer reaches of the metropolitan region.

---

My friend Tim and I used to hit golf balls into the water from the shoreline of lower Manhattan. Tim ordered the balls by the gross, used, from a golfing magazine; they had scuffs, smiles, spray-painted dots, and legends like "Tri-County Challenge—'80" and "Lost by Dan Trivino" and "Molub-Alloy The Metallic Lubricant" and "Maintenance Supply Co. Huntersville N.C." We told ourselves we were working on our drives. All we needed was a place open to the water; usually, we could find cracks in the asphalt or concrete big enough to fit a tee. We picked our targets. Once, I tried to land a ball on a mattress going out with the tide on the East River. I didn't succeed, but it would have been cool if I had. Once, I bounced a flat, hard drive off the stone base of the nearer tower of the Manhattan Bridge. A following shot struck the inside of an immense, upreaching I-beam, ricocheted to the opposite inside, then sped diagonally down into the water. Tim hit a beauty across a dredged inlet by a construction site at Battery Park City, the ball socking into a distant pile of sand and burying itself in a small landslide. One that he aimed at a passing container ship fell just short of the hull with a white exclamation point of a splash. My best shot came from a pier on the Lower East Side one winter morning with five inches of snow on the ground. Placing the ball on snow had a psychological effect on me, and I hit perfect drive after perfect drive. A cargo ship came along, well out in the channel. I took careful aim, kept my head down, and stroked one of those unstoppable balls that seem to rise like music, octave by octave—would it hit that glass housing near the bow? would they call the Coast Guard?—as the ship moved but not fast enough: ship and ball intersected, and a puff of snow came from a metal hatch cover amidships. Half a second later, we heard the impact's muffled clang. The name of the vessel was the *John B. Carroll*.

Just after dawn one day, we were hitting off an abandoned pier by Rutgers Slip, upstream from the Manhattan Bridge, when a little guy who had been sitting there on a folding metal chair came over and began to talk to us. Pointing to the water, he said, "See that? Those're anchovies. Like you put on pizza." Until then, I had never looked closely at the water of the East River—assuming the worst about it, I suppose—but now I observed that it was indeed full of silver-sided bait fish swirling and boiling like noodles in soup. The school was thick down as deep as you could see. The guy continued to talk about anchovies and other subjects as we continued to hit. He had a hand line with what looked like a piece of lime-green surgical tubing for a lure. When he left, he picked up from among some broken pallets a big striped bass he had caught. We had not noticed the fish before. He carried it off—to sell in Chinatown, he said—by a scrap of plastic packing rope strung through its mouth and gills.

Soon after that, we saw in the *Times* that the International Maritime Organization had issued a prohibition against ocean dumping of non-biodegradable plastics—a category that would include golf balls. To protect sea life, the ruling applied to all oceangoing vessels, and to cruise ships' profitable practice of selling golf balls for passengers to hit. We had suspected that what we were doing qualified as minor vandalism; now, thanks to the I.M.O., we were sure. So we stopped (there is now a net-enclosed driving range on one of the Hudson River piers we used to use), and I began to think more about the guy with the striped bass. I had read about stripers—the game fish that can grow to fifty or sixty pounds or more, the trophy species sought by thousands of oilskin-clad surf anglers, the voracious schooling fish that sometimes chase mullet and menhaden and tinker mackerel up onto the beach, the anadromous swimmer that lives most of its life in the ocean and spawns locally in the Hudson River—but I never fished for them.

I began to scout up and down the shoreline in Manhattan on bright fall afternoons. At a rotted wooden pipe that had the appearance of a large barrel extending into the East River at Twentieth Street, I saw alewives nosing against moss-covered pilings. More bait appeared in the semi-clear water in sudden relief against the dark background of a drowned car seat. In fact, from Twenty-third Street all the way down to the tip of Corlears Hook, just south of Grand Street, the East River depths glinted with shifting schools of bait. All the books say that where there's bait there are stripers. I bought a nine-foot surf-casting rod and a spinning reel with twenty-pound-test line. I bought one-ounce white leadhead jigs with tails of white bucktail hair, and other lures. Stripers are known to move at dawn, to feed by first light. I woke up at four one morning and took the subway to Manhattan from my apartment, in Brooklyn—the first time I had ever approached a fish by going under it. "Striped bass," the token-booth clerk said when he saw my fishing rod. I rode with transit workers in orange-mesh vests carrying sacks of tokens and accompanied by armed guards, got off at the East Broadway stop, and walked down to the East River in the late night of Chinatown. A starling's raspy cry startled me. Police cars idled; clouds of steam from a steam tunnel crossed the street.

At the southern end of Corlears Hook Park is a graffiti-covered brick structure about the size of a shed, which extends into the river. The structure has no windows—only metal vents on two sides. Maybe it is part of an airshaft for an underwater tunnel. Warm air comes from the vents sometimes, and people who fish here call the structure the Heat House. A good cast from the Heat House's concrete apron can reach a tidal rip that forms on water ebbing around this corner of Manhattan Island. I set up my rod and tied on a lure by the light of a street light and went through a break in a chain-link fence. A man was sleeping on the concrete behind the Heat House, however, in the warm air from the vents. He had one shoe on, the other beneath his head. I moved to the walkway along the river upstream and began to fish there. The bottom of the river must be a cluttered spot—I hung up lure after lure. At first light, gulls began to fly by. I heard the rattle of shopping-cart wheels as a bottle-and-can-collecting guy appeared. The man behind the Heat House woke up and left, and I took his place. I was casting the bucktail jig about fifty yards to the tide rip, retrieving with short, quick pulls. Truck traffic on the Manhattan Bridge had slowed to a standstill, and on the bridge's lower level the bright beads of the D-train windows slid back and forth. Occasional passing barges sent wakes sloshing along the shore. The first jogger went by, singing tonelessly with his Walkman. At almost the moment of sunrise, about four minutes past seven, I felt a strong resistance on my line. I thought at first that I was hung up again. Then the resistance began to move. I pumped and reeled, gaining line. I still wasn't sure what I would pull out of there—an infant car seat, say, would have been only a mild surprise. But then the resistance was pulling, jerking. In the murky water I saw a flash of white, then stripes—a striper! It was about two feet long, and bent my rod double as I tried to hoist it out. Then there it was, slapping around on the concrete.

Striped bass are in many respects the perfect New York fish. They go well with the look of downtown. They are, for starters, pin-striped; the lines along their sides are black fading to light cobalt blue at the edges. The dime-size silver scales look newly minted, and there is an urban glint to the eye and a mobility to the wide predator jaw. If they could talk, they would talk fast. Although really big stripers take on a no-neck, thuggish, rectangular look, ones this size are classically proportioned—fish a child would draw. I unhooked mine and picked it up with both hands. All muscle, it writhed; a sharp spine of the dorsal fin went into my hand, and—thump, bump—the fish was back in the water and gone. A woman jogger doing leg-stretching exercises on the fence looked at me unsmiling, as if I were a fish abuser. Generally, when I fish I am in the woods, standing in weeds or mud or sand. Hauling a fish into the city like this made both city and fish more vivid—as if a striped bass had suddenly arrived flopping on my desk. A few casts later, I hooked another. It was about the same size but fought harder, and I had more trouble getting the hook out. Scales scraped off on the concrete as I held the fish down. I was too high up to reach the water, and so could not rinse the slime from my hands. I let the fish go; here a striper must be thirty-six inches long before you can keep it. (Also, because of the danger of contamination from PCBs and other chemicals, the State Department of Health recommends that people eat little or no fish caught in New York Harbor.) I broke down my rod and walked back to the subway and got home in time to take my daughter to school.

I wanted to catch more and bigger stripers. I got striper fever. I read outdoor columns about stripers in newspapers and picked up angling newsletters in tackle shops and called recorded fishing tapes at a dollar forty-five a minute and talked to closemouthed striper anglers. In a tackle store in Bay Ridge, several striper anglers trading stories dropped their voices and leaned toward one another as I approached. Striper anglers have big, gill-like necks, wear clothing in layers, and yawn ostentatiously in daylight. They are famous for their divorce rate; the striper is a night creature, and its pursuers must be, too. I fished for stripers all this fall. Mostly, I went to Sandy Hook, the expanse of barrier beach bent like a crooked arm from the Jersey shore at the southern approach to New York Harbor. Sandy Hook is visible from Brooklyn, and from Sandy Hook you can see the Verrazano Narrows Bridge, the World Trade towers, and the sunrise on the windows of apartment buildings in Brighton Beach. People have caught many big stripers at Sandy Hook; it is among the prime striper-fishing grounds on the East Coast.

I knew nothing about fishing in surf. At first, it feels funny to park in a beach parking lot (Sandy Hook's beaches are all part of a national recreation area), put on chest waders, rig up, walk to an ocean stretching thousands of miles to Spain, and cast. My first day, I fished along the beach for several miles, using a swimming plug bigger than many trout I've been happy to catch. Casting it was hard work. I didn't know for sure how far into the ocean I should wade. A big wave knocked me down onto one arm. I climbed back on the beach and saw a sign in the distance. I thought perhaps it warned of dangerous surf. I walked over to it. It said:

## ATTENTION.
## BEYOND THIS POINT
## YOU MAY ENCOUNTER
## NUDE SUNBATHERS

The wind was blowing hard, lifting sand in smoky wraiths and rattling it against pieces of plastic trash. A half-buried strip of photographic film flapped rapidly with an industrial sound; it had dug a sharp-edged trench beside itself. The temperature was about fifty degrees—not nude-sunbathing weather. As I continued, however, I passed a trim bronze naked guy accompanying a clothed female, then a trio of old guys strolling along in hats, sweatshirts, dark glasses, sneakers, knee socks, and no pants. One guy said hello, I said hello back.

Mostly, I fished in the hours just before and after dawn. Sandy Hook, maybe twelve air miles from my apartment, is about an hour and a quarter away by car. I drove across Staten Island and through Jersey in light traffic, listening to radio programs with few commercials, sometimes following into a toll booth the four-wheel-drive vehicle of another striper angler. The millions in their beds on a full-moon night in October may not know that the beaches nearby are lined with hundreds of striper anglers, mostly men but some women, looking seaward as if awaiting an invasion. Darkness makes them more solitary. Anglers rig up by their cars' overhead lights and walk to the beach thirty feet apart in silence. I passed many anglers in the dark but never exchanged a word. When you can't really see the ocean, you hear it and smell it more. On clear mornings, dawn came up full and sudden, like houselights in a theatre, and the sun followed along behind. Venus was bright on the horizon to the northeast at 5 A.M. On cloudy mornings, dawn was dull, with occasional surprises: a red sun would pop up on the horizon, chin itself on a low ceiling of gray, and disappear for good; or, though the horizon stayed dark, silvery light would glisten on the water, and from a break in the clouds, celestially high, beams from the sunrise would spill down.

Sometimes the waves were like high hedges. Sometimes the sea just sat there and swayed; then, all of a sudden, a breaker would *whump* and the foam would be up under my arms. I cast and reeled, cast and reeled. A moment came when I could see my lure in the air as I cast, and a later moment when I could make out its succinct splash. The birds woke. If the tide was going out, gulls by the thousand occupied the exposed sand. A gull picked up a clam, dropped it to break the shell, failed, and kept on trying. Flocks of little gray-and-white shorebirds—sanderlings?—stayed right at the waves' edges. Long combers ran the birds back up the beach like the flat of a hand pushing crumbs. As waves rolled to the shore, they made white broken shells on the bottom hop up into them with a sort of vacuum-cleaner effect. Pieces of shells bounced from the waves' tops. I sometimes hooked a shell or a piece of clam but (at first) no fish of any kind. After full daylight, the anglers began to give up and came walking back to their cars. They wore yellow slickers, red-and-black checked hunting caps, camouflage coveralls, Penn State sweatshirts. At the ends of their lines dangled swimming plugs, popping plugs, rigged eels, sandworms, bloodworms, gobs of clams the size of base-balls. Some guys said the fish weren't here yet, or the mullet hadn't arrived to draw them, or the water was too murky or still too warm.

One morning, I brought peanut-butter-and-jelly sandwiches and bottled water, and stayed. By eight-thirty, along the whole expanse of beach I could see only one other angler. As I watched, his rod bent. I walked toward him and saw him land a big fish and let it go. When I got near, I began to cast. I had switched to the same leadhead jig that had worked in the East River; most of the white paint had been scraped off it by now. At once, I felt a hard, unmistakable hit, and the line went tight. Briefly, the fish took line, and, briefly, I hoped it would be big. The line was going right into the near-vertical side of a wave; at the base of a following wave I saw a swirl from the tail. I backed up the beach and slid the fish out of the foam and into a rivulet the ebbing tide had cut in the sand. It was a striper, good-sized but still not legal, hooked at the hinge of the jaw. I held it up and the other angler yelled, "Way to go!" I set it back in the surf.

At a tackle store in nearby Atlantic Highlands, amid sand spikes to hold rods on the beach, lead-loaded priests for clubbing fish, spiked cleats for climbing on jetties, bottles of fish scent to spray on lures, basins of wildly wriggling eels, and snapshots of stripers bigger than a six-year-old child, I talked to a veteran striper angler named Frank. He worked there and had caught some of the fish in the pictures. He gave me a number of tips, among them the fact that stripers love bad weather—the worse the weather, the more the stripers like it. As a result, one afternoon I fished in a storm that descended from the north, covering the city and its lights like a fire blanket. I had to adjust my hat to the tightest fit, and when the rain hit my eyes it hurt. Wind blew spray from the wave crests like dust behind a car, and it rolled pieces of foam along the sand, where they dwindled in a blink. Whitish-brown foam covered the sea farther out than I could cast. Near some sunken rocks, I lost a lure, and accidentally put my next cast in the same spot. Reeling in fast to stay off the bottom, I felt a hard tug. The line started moving up the beach, I went with it, and the next thing I knew I had a striper on the sand at my feet. I hardly looked at it, in all the rain and spray: it was like something blown in by the storm, like a fish left in somebody's pants after a dousing in a cartoon. And, unfortunately, it was another "short," as the striper anglers call them. The bells of a buoy clanged and clanged. On the dim horizon, in the Ambrose Channel, a three-masted sailing ship in silhouette slowly headed for New York.

The striped bass never did show up in any numbers in the surf at Sandy Hook this fall, as near as I can tell. Striper anglers stood in the parking lots with their waders folded down around their middles and groused. Guys trudging back from the surf through the beach-plum bushes had similar expressions of frustration. A few talked about last year, or another year, and how the stripers were chasing bunkers in the wash at their feet, how the bluefish ate until the bait was coming out of their mouths, how some mornings every guy came home with a fish. This year, striper fishing was said to be good in the surf at Montauk, and in Staten Island Bay, and at Cape May, farther south in Jersey. But not, for some reason, here.

Striper season on the coast of New Jersey remains open all winter. The wind was blowing trash cans around on my street the last time I went out. On the Verrazano Bridge at 4 A.M., the car felt like a plane flying in turbulence. Street signs were shaking back and forth and flashing their reflections. As soon as I turned onto the road that runs along Sandy Hook, salt spray began to streak the windshield. I drove slowly down to Parking Area F, and as I got close my headlights picked out the waves lurching from the dark like shrouded beings in a horror movie. They were mobbing the beach: there was no beach—just waves breaking so fast as to have no rhythm at all. The wind was trying to shout them down. I walked to take a closer look, and a speedy long surge chased me back. I decided I wanted to be in the car. As I backed out, a comber broke over the sand barrier and came down into the parking lot. I turned up the car heater and headed for home. People say the stripers will return again in May.

# 18

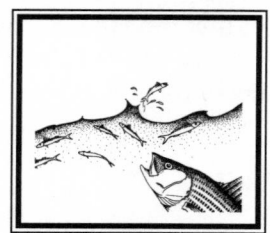

# Growing Up with *Roccus*

Dan Levin

F| or some individuals, striper fishing begins as a burst of passion, only to evolve into a familiar and stable refuge from life's afflictions. Sparked as a boy by magazine articles on stripers and the sight of casters in the surf, in Growing Up with Roccus (1967), Levin courses from the wildly enthusiastic futility of youth to the proficiency of adulthood, tracing his development as a striped bass angler against the broader backdrop of his life.

---

In coastal waters from Eastport to Long Island, a striped, silver-coated heartbreaker named *Roccus Saxatilis* is king. Those who go down to the sea with rod and reel know him as Mr. Striped Bass, or Striper, and each year thousands of otherwise normal human beings succumb to his charms. To get *Roccus* on the end of a line, men have neglected their health, ignored their families, and even jeopardized promising careers. In spite of all the ardor cast in his direction, *Roccus* doesn't seem to care. He can show such a remarkable disinclination to being caught that some men have labored half a lifetime to land him flopping and kicking at their feet.

I was lucky though. It only took me 11 years. My moment of truth came in September of 1960, on the banks of the Cape Cod Canal. Though that first bass weighed only six pounds, I knew that were I to catch a thousand more it would never again be quite the same. I walked back to my car that day grinning and displaying my fish like a barefoot boy, thinking of how this madness had all begun.

For the first six or seven years of my fishing career I didn't know a Striped Bass from a Pickled Herring. Fishing was fun. I usually went in the afternoon and came home before dark. Huck Finn had the Mississippi River, and I had the rocks and tide pools of Nahant, Massachusetts, a rocky peninsula just north of Boston where my family spent its summers. Zane Grey wouldn't have written about my adventures, but I doubt if even he ever caught 63 cunners at one sitting, as I did one memorable afternoon from the old town pier. My fishing thrills were scaled to the tastes of a small boy. There were no Atlantic salmon where I fished, but I was a pretty delighted nine-year-old the evening I caught three gleaming pollack that jumped clear of the water. My family didn't demand swordfish; they greeted me like a hero the day I paraded down the street with a five pound cod. By the summer of 1950, however, the days of this youthful fishing idyll were numbered.

Walking down the beach one evening in early August of that year, I noticed two men standing waist deep in the water, casting with long rods. I'd never seen anyone fishing from the beach before. A neighbor was watching them from the seawall, and I asked him what they were fishing for. "I guess it's those Stripers," he said. "Stripers?" I replied, my eyes opening wide. "Stripers!" I thought. Visions of great, silvery, striped fish came back to me from the magazines I'd begun to read avidly. Such exotics had never seemed to be part of my world.

Next morning, as if timed to compound my excitement, the local paper ran a picture of a 45-pound Striper caught two nights earlier by a fisherman trolling just off the beach. That afternoon I blew most of my allowance on the same color and brand of plug the bass had been caught on. I broke out my only heavy outfit: a stubby boat rod with reel to match.

Two friends across the street had a boat and motor, and when I showed them the picture of the fish and they saw how smitten I was, they agreed to take me out that evening. By the time we began the short run to the fishing grounds I'd oiled my reel three times. With

my fisherman's imagination working overtime, every eddy or slapping of wave against rock in the darkening water was the swirl of a
giant Striper. About 200 yards from the beach, we turned parallel to
the surf and I began paying out line. For the next two hours I stared
into the dark, waiting tensely for what I was sure would be the strike
of a world record Striped Bass, fully expecting to be yanked overboard when it came.

There was no Striper that night or on two other nights of trolling
in the next two weeks. After the third trip, during which we were almost swamped by a comber that loomed up in the dark directly over
our heads, my friends had lost their enthusiasm for Striper fishing.
For the rest of that summer I fished for *Roccus* from shore. What
nights of misery!

It's possible that I didn't come within 12 miles of a Striper; that
45-pounder may have been taken from someone's wall. Besides, I
didn't have the right tackle. Trying to cast with that boat rod was like
trying to pole vault with a broomstick. If they'd kept records for such
things, I might have gone into the books on any of my trips with the
world's worst backlash. Each night I'd drag myself home to the
kitchen table, where the whole family would make a game of untangling my line. Finally, after more than a dozen chilly, wet, bassless
evenings, I retired for lengthy contemplation of my strategy. I had
never even seen a Striped Bass, even in a fish market, and I began to
wonder if the species had been dreamed up by some press agent trying to sell fishing tackle.

According to the Boston papers, in the summer of 1952, Stripers
were swarming all around Cape Cod and Plum Island, the latter little
more than an hour's drive away. Once again I enlisted the aid of
neighbors to help further my fishing career. I think they were afraid
to refuse me; I had a strange look in my eyes.

On a Friday evening in July, we filled their car with sandwiches
and fishing tackle and headed toward Striper territory. I carefully
made sure that their trunk was wide enough to accommodate a
Striper of at least 30 pounds. At sundown I stood on a high bluff, disappointed and a little surprised not to see schools of bass breaking all
the way to the horizon.

I set up my new casting rod in record time and waded into the
surf, undaunted by unseasonably cold weather. After five casts and
three backlashes brought on by nearly frozen fingers and the anticipation of my first Striper, it began to pour, and soon I couldn't see

through my rain-streaked glasses. I had no foul weather gear, and after about five minutes of shivering I ran for the car to sit out the storm. For the rest of the night I sat in the back seat like a pickled eel, soaked and salty, wedged between bags of sandwiches and tackle boxes. About dawn the rain slowed to a miserable drizzle, and when I got out to stretch a truck pulled up beside us in the parking lot. "Anything doing?" the driver asked from the cab.

"Are you kidding?" I replied. "I'll bet there isn't a bass in miles."

"I've got one," he said matter-of-factly, beckoning to the back of the truck.

It seemed a cruel joke but I looked anyway. My jaw dropped and I stood transfixed. There, before my unbelieving eyes, was a prime specimen of Striped Basshood. "Twenty-nine pounds," the driver called back to me. I walked around it and around it, pressing on the gills, pulling on the fins, rubbing its shiny sides, and hefting its broad tail. I asked the fisherman about 50 questions, but it was obvious that he was very blase' about the whole thing.

"How did he fight?" I asked, expecting to hear him tell of an hour-long battle during which he was almost pulled out to sea at least a dozen times.

"Oh, you know they're on," he replied nonchalantly; "They put a bend in the rod." It had begun to rain again, hard as before, and I said goodbye to the bass fisherman and got back onto the car.

My only contacts with *Roccus* in the next two years were three or four less-than-thrilling encounters in fish markets, and in romantic daydreams where I always pictured myself landing a world record bass and then heroically releasing it to fight another day. I didn't own a car; but in mid-September of 1955 I talked my family into a short vacation at a place storied in Striper annals, Nauset Beach on outer Cape Cod. Nauset is a magnificent stretch of surf-pounded, barrier beach, and many big bass are taken there each year. On the wall of a building near the beach, I discovered a sign which read:

Largest Striped Bass—109 lbs. Emerson Sparrow used a 6 oz. pewter drail on a cod line hand cast from the beach May 30, 1888.

Since the rod and reel record for Striped Bass is only 73 pounds, this inspired me to no end, and I fished for three days and most of three nights without a strike. On the third day I headed for a nearby trout pond. I returned to the motel about four hours later, glanced into the back of the owner's pickup truck, and let out a whoop. There lay a three-foot-deep pile of Stripers, none less than 35 pounds. As I stood there open-mouthed, the fisherman came out, grinning. "We tried to find you, but you'd left," he said. "That school was within spitting distance of the beach for more than an hour." Gesturing to a broken surf rod leaning against the truck, he added ruefully, "That was a world record bass, I'm sure; and I thought I'd stop him by tightening up on the drag."

It was about this time that I became interested in another species: warm-blooded, long-haired, and finless; and although I managed to get away on many short fishing jaunts in the next four years, my Striper fishing suffered. Unlike *Roccus*, these longhairs were all over the place, and I managed to land a few. But by 1959, the novelty was wearing off, and in spite of dates, college classes, and summer jobs, I was bass fishing again. When I caught that first bass a year later, it seemed as much a personal milestone as my first case of puppy love or my high school graduation; now I was a pro.

As spring warmed into summer in 1962, I readied my tackle with new confidence; anything was possible now. One afternoon that July, I hauled three Stripers out of the Merrimac River at Newburyport, one a seven-pounder. What's more, as I kneeled on the beach cleaning my catch, a group of tourists asked me how they could catch Stripers too; now I was an authority. I answered nonchalantly, of course drawing on the vast store of knowledge gained in personally landing four bass in 12 years. Naturally they were impressed. I toyed with the idea of becoming a professional guide.

With the purchase of my first car the next summer, and the increased mobility it would offer, I knew that my eventual enshrinement in the Fishing Hall of Fame was assured.

My first trip of that year, in June, revealed one of the basic truths about Striper fishing: you don't have to catch anything to have a memorable time. It was dusk when I arrived at Plum Island, and since my favorite stretch of shore was lined with fishermen, I decided to postpone my fishing until dawn and sack out at the foot of a sand dune. After digging, patting down, and tossing for more than two hours, I got comfortable and began to doze off. It seemed like a dream minutes later when four shadowy figures, talking loudly, approached from the direction of the beach. A moment later I knew I wasn't dreaming. A large, booted foot was standing on my hand and another was on the foot of my sleeping bag. A third foot was prodding me fairly solidly in the ribs. Still groggy, I looked up; and although it was a very dark night I made out four men standing over me, all wearing boot-foot, chest-high waders. "I don't know what it is," one said. "Cripes, it looks like a body," another added.

By this time I was fully awake. "It *is* a body, you donkey!" I replied caustically. They must have been pretty embarrassed, because they walked away without saying anything. For the rest of the night, between searching for a safe place to sleep and trying to get comfortable again, I managed to sleep about an hour. I didn't feel much like fishing when the first rays of light appeared in the sky; so I got in my car and drove home.

Despite its slapstick beginnings, that season proved a successful one. More than a dozen years of frustrating trial and error had begun paying off. Now I had the appropriate tackle, and knew a great deal about baits and lures and tides. What's more, I was mobile; at a moment's notice I could jump into my own car and head confidently to the Cape Cod Canal, Plum Island, or some other favorite spot. Gone forever was the barefoot boy with the tangled line, trudging home wet and tired in the dark.

On a dark night late in September, alone in a skiff on Scituate's North River, I netted an eight-pound bass, the largest I'd ever caught. A week later, in the middle of a bright October afternoon, know-how and luck combined to give me my greatest catch: seven bass in less than two hours of fishing in Sandwich Creek, a Cape Cod tidal stream. But fishing isn't a game of statistics; what is most memorable is rarely how many fish or how big. It was more than just the hope of catching that first Striper that drove me back to the beaches through all those years of vain pursuit; always there was the eerie beauty of the nighttime surf; the way the sun rose over the lonely beach at dawn, with the waves rolling in to break cool and creaming around my bare legs; and how good it was to be alone with my thoughts, with only the clean smell of the salt air, the crying of the gulls, and the next cast . . . always that next cast.

Seventeen summers have passed since that night I first fell under *Roccus's* magic spell. For two or three seasons now business obligations and a busy social life have limited my fishing to an occasional, spur-of-the-moment afternoon or evening; but still, each year has produced at least a few Stripers. Fishing has become more of a game; there are friendly rivalries and small bets over who will catch the season's first or biggest bass. Somewhere though, somehow, that sense of boyish wonder that began it all has gone astray. Or has it? Something that happened early this year in a Boston fish store got me wondering. I have always loved fish stores, and on a bright day in the last week of March my favorite one had six or seven small Stripers on ice in the window. I stuck my head through the doorway. "Where are they from?" I asked the proprietor, pointing to the bass.

"New Jersey," he replied.

"They're on their way north," I thought. I went back to the window and for a long time I gazed at the bass and thought of those nights on Nahant Beach when I was 12. Then I rushed home and put a new coat of varnish on an old surf rod.

# 19

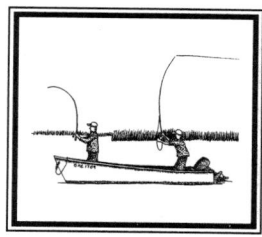

# Menemsha Bight: Bass Derby

Red Smith

T he shores of Martha's Vineyard, a scenic island within view of Cape
Cod, are a haven for stripers. The annual, month-long Martha's
Vineyard Striped Bass and Bluefish Derby began in 1946; in 1985 stripers
were removed from the tournament as a symbolic gesture toward conser-
vation of their declining stocks. Derby contestants from afar competed with
locals for prizes that over the years have included boats, cars, a hunting
lodge, canned hams, a case of peas, chopsticks, and the prestige that attends
weighing-in the largest bass caught by among some of the most expert
anglers ever to pursue the fish. Red Smith, better known for his writing on
team sports, also was an accomplished fisherman. In Menemsha Bight:
Bass Derby (1963), Smith takes a light-hearted look at the Derby scene.

The rain which had been falling in sudden sullen bursts all day
backed off just before the arrival of Mr. Al Brickman, proprietor of
Vineyard Haven's popular stores, Abercrombie & Brickman and
Bergdorf-Brickman. Mr. Brickman had contracted to show an ignora-
mus a thing or two about fishing in the annual Martha's Vineyard
striped bass derby, a month-long competition in which anglers who

snatch the largest comestibles out of the oceans are rewarded with automobiles, cruisers, fishing tackle, etc.

Mr. Brickman was accompanied by Stan Bryden, an island man, and General Charles W. Ryder, who recently switched his address from one island, Japan, to another island, Martha's Vineyard. On the drive down to Menemsha Bight, all three explained that experience of surf casting was not essential to a derby candidate.

"That boy Drake," said Stan Bryden, "whose forty-pounder is leading the field right now, never caught a bass before he hooked this one."

"One day," said Al Brickman, "there was an off-island kid over here on his honeymoon, borrowed some tackle and made one cast and got a backlash. While he was untangling the backlash, a bass took his plug. He couldn't reel in so he just backed up inland and dragged the bass onto the beach. He lost the plug, and that night he come down to my store, bought another plug, went back and caught another striper."

At Menemsha Bight the bass-slayers got into hip boots and rubberized overalls and waterproofed parkas and lugged their tackle down to the beach. The tide was rampaging out through a narrow cut and there were perhaps half a dozen fishermen casting into the current from the rock jetty, with a dozen or so more strung out along the beach flinging their feathered jigs into the surf. The jigs, or plugs, or tin squids, are cigar-sized gobbets of lead with feather tails which, it is optimistically hoped, will look edible to large stupid fish.

Either there weren't any large fish or they weren't stupid enough. The anglers kept heaving their jigs out to sea and reeling them in and nothing else kept happening. Nobody worked too hard. A guy would make a few fruitless casts, then thrust the butt of his rod into the sand and go light up a cigarette and tell some lies.

"When I was a kid," Al Brickman was saying, "a buddy and I used to camp down here in two pup tents and go fishing, and the things we'd catch you wouldn't believe. Ever see a goose fish? They have two feet on 'em webbed just like geese."

"See old Levi Jackson fishing down the beach there?" said Ted Henley, an island man. "Every time I see him I think of one time I saw him with a monkfish, which are as fat as this with a mouth that big. He'd stuffed this monkfish full of rocks and old scrap iron and all sorts of heavy stuff and then I saw him sewing up the fish's big mouth. I watched, wondering what in the world he could be doing.

"Well, he finally got the fish sewed up and then he picked it up like this and threw it overboard. I heard him say, 'There, you slob. You've torn up my nets enough. You'll never do it to anybody else.' "

A gull flew in from sea, wobbling crookedly, with something dangling from its claws. The bird alighted on the jetty close enough so you could see it had a surf-casting plug looped to one foot. Apparently it had been stupid enough to think this gadget of lead and feather was a fish.

"I'm going to get that jig," Ted Henley said, and he picked up a stone and crept toward the bird. When he got close he threw the rock. It missed, but the gull took flight with a scream and the plug shook free and Ted recovered it.

The tide was changing and bluefish were breaking water in the rollers out beyond the reach of the beach casters. Now one of them hooked into a fish and a man beside him shouted, pointing, and all the yarn-spinners snatched up their rods and rushed to the water's edge and began casting relentlessly. Nobody got anything, except the one man who had brought in a bluefish.

As evening came on, more cars rolled down to the beach and more fishermen went to work. When the setting sun broke through clouds on the horizon there were about twenty-five anglers strung along the beach casting earnestly. Some of them would keep at it all night.

Al Brickman's party stowed tackle and started for home. General Ryder was telling about bass-fishing in the spring in Menemsha Pond during the spawning run of herring. The herring, he said, come through a cut from the ocean and go into the pond to spawn and the stripers follow them in.

"You net some herring," he said, "and put one on your line for bait, hooking it through the fleshy part of the back. Then you toss him out and teach him to swim. A bass comes along and slaps the herring, stunning him. You wait, because the bass will then go around and try to eat him head on. When the bass takes the herring in his mouth and starts swimming away, you tighten your reel and you have him.

"The gulls, though, they come in with the bass and they hang up there waiting. When a bass stuns a herring, the gull dives and grabs the stunned bait. Then you've got a gull in the air on the end of your line, and that's something."

"Did you see cormorant-fishing in the Orient?" the general was asked.

"You mean where they have a cormorant with a ring around his neck so he can't swallow the fish, and they send the bird out fishing and he grabs the fish and they take it away from him? Yes," the general said, "I saw it and the cormorants love it. They get to eat the little fish, which slip down their throats."

"I have also," the general said, "netted ducks in the private preserves of the Emperor of Japan. You use a long-handled net and catch the ducks on the wing. That's quite a sport too."

That's what a bass derby is like. No bass, but much education.

# 20

# Surf Fishing: The Nighttime Provides an Edge

*Nelson Bryant*

T| he striped bass is lord of the nighttime shallows, riding the currents
and arrowing through tide rips to strike passing prey. Although some
anglers enjoy a modicum of success with stripers in daylight, it is those
who time their efforts to the fish's nocturnal forays who experience the most
consistent catches. Nelson Bryant ruminates on moon phases, tides, and
the advantages to the surfcaster in mastering night fishing in Surf Fishing:
The Nighttime Provides an Edge.

Surf fishermen who cherish the evening cocktail hour or who feel
they must eat every supper with family or friends should turn to ten-
nis. With striped bass—and, to a lesser degree, bluefish—the very
best time to be abroad is at sundown and thereafter.

Indeed, it is this urge to leave the beach for familial bliss or the
tinkling of ice in tall glasses evinced by so many that makes it possible for me to keep visiting the increasingly crowded beaches of the
Northeast for a bit of angling. God bless gin and tonic, inane chatter
and, though I risk sounding like an ogre, togetherness. Again and
again, after virtually all the four-wheel-drive vehicles have ground

their way into the sunset, and the bright boats off shore are cutting their full-throttle wakes for the dock, the fish arrive.

Although I have fished the salt water off every state from Maine to Florida, my surf angling south of Long Island has not been sufficiently intensive to permit me to extend my generalizations to areas beyond. I know only that on Cape Cod and its outlying islands, and on the south side of Long Island, my remarks about surf fishing are valid.

Stripers in particular do a great deal of feeding after dark. Bluefish forage at night also—witness the success of party boats out of New Jersey that chum for them off shore on summer evenings. One can usually, if they are running in any significant numbers at all, catch all the blues one wants during the day. Still, dusk can be the most productive time.

Some years ago, as I angled a stretch of Sound shore where I could consistently catch striped bass at night but not in the daytime, it occurred to me that the fish might be there in the day but simply not feeding.

For three straight days, I snorkeled up and down the beach, covering more than a mile each time and ranging from 20 yards off shore to more than 150. I saw fewer than half a dozen stripers during those swims, but each evening after sunset the fish were responding to my surface swimming plugs.

I have a theory, though no way to substantiate it, that the striped bass's dislike of shallow water—by this I mean anything from 2 to 10 feet deep—is born of his days as a juvenile, when, only a few inches long, he was pursued by predatory fish, from which he tried to escape in the shallows, only to be harried from above by terns and gulls. At night, there was no danger of attack from above. At night, the striper can move, without this residual fear, in shore, in search of two of his favorite food fish—the sand eel and the silverside minnow. Also, of course, certain marine worms upon which the stripers feed are nocturnal.

Whatever the reason for this behavior, you will often find the stripers at night in areas they totally eschew during the daytime.

I know, for example, of two extensive sand bars off Chappaquiddick Island where, during a very low tide, a big bass would have trouble keeping wet. Yet large fish frequent these places at night, making them ideal for wading fishermen, including the fly rodder.

And, just to make this situation a bit more complicated, I have often been able to raise, but not hook, striped bass along a rocky beach during the daylight, and then, at dusk or dark, to catch all I wanted in the same spot.

For years, I thought that a rising tide at night was the best situation for shore fishing for striped bass, but in the past decade this theory has proved a bit wobbly. Movements of fish and baitfish change, and one must be constantly on guard against a rote approach. Experiment constantly with timing and technique, and remember to glean whatever information you can from fellow anglers. There is no substitute for local knowledge of an area.

Night surf-casting requires a reasonable level of expertise. If you are a beginner, practice during the daylight until you know precisely where your lure is going each time you cast it. If—though it isn't likely—you are trying to master casting with a conventional revolving spool reel rather than a spinning reel, you must, before you venture forth in the dark, have reached the point where backlashes are virtually a thing of the past.

And if there are other anglers nearby at night, keep an eye open for them and make sure you don't hook them on your back-cast. This is particularly true when you're fly fishing, for 60 or 70 feet of line may be unrolling behind you.

Also, carry a light so that you can change lures, inspect lures for weed and remove lures from fish.

Someday I'm going to purchase one of those little penlights with a flexible neck and clip for a pocket I see advertised in fly-fishing magazines, but until I do I'll get by with a tiny disposable light, the kind a lady drops into her purse. It throws enough of a beam to do the jobs mentioned above and is small enough so I can hold it in my mouth and work with both hands. I dislike anything that is disposable, because in using it I am lending impetus to a waste-oriented culture. But total consistency is boring.

During the summer in the Northeast, I am quite comfortable at night in nothing but sneakers, shorts and shirt, but some anglers dislike remaining wet for long periods and use waders.

Your tackle box need be nothing more than a musette bag with half a dozen lures and a small hand gaff, although there are little over-the-shoulder bags with separate plastic-lined compartments designed for the surf fishermen.

The popping plug is a splendid lure to use on both stripers and bluefish. It is particularly effective with the latter, because—as with the fly fisherman's floating fly—one can see the strike. It is my belief that one has better luck with a surface or a subsurface swimmer after dark.

One sometimes hears surf fishermen discussing whether a bright moon hinders angling success. I have no strong feelings on this, even though many years ago I read something by Jacques Cousteau, which was, I think, attributed to Mediterranean commercial fishermen, to the effect that when the moon is full, the sea is empty of fish.

I have taken more striped bass on dark nights than on bright ones but have also done more fishing on such evenings. I have also caught stripers on the full of the moon, when I could see the wakes of the big fish as they moved up behind the plug in the shallow waters of a bay.

If you have the bent for it—I have tried, but failed miserably— keep a log of your night fishing endeavors. List the time, the tide and the phase of the moon, and add solid information of a similar nature from reputable anglers. If you could do this for several years, you might discover something of value, but don't be distressed if the fish don't cooperate. Their world is one of raw survival—of opportunistic behavior, of endeavoring to find the most food with the least energy expended—and it is constantly changing, however subtly.

And, as an addendum to the Mediterranean quotation, remember that when a surf fisherman's glass and stomach are full, his freezer will be empty.

# 21

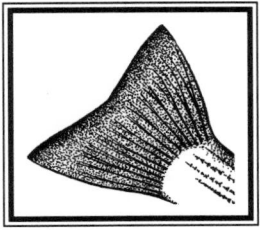

# No Wind in the Willows

Russell Chatham

*T he average driver crossing a coastal bridge has no conception of what lurks under its arches. But the abutments of bridges are to stripers what cribs and wing dams are to trout—manmade structures that provide exquisite cover to ambush whatever forage the realigned and sharpened currents bring them. In No Wind in the Willows (1990), Russell Chatham describes the pleasures and peculiarities of flyfishing for striped bass near a bridge spanning the backwaters of San Francisco Bay.*

Outside a blizzard is raging, and the familiar edges that normally define my yard, with its fences, woodpile, and barns, have long vanished beneath the snow. My house, the last on an unpaved road among aspen and pine forests along the northwestern perimeter of Montana's vast Absaroka wilderness, is well on its way toward becoming a smallish speck on the surface of a preposterous marshmallow.

I'm unable to go out, and as I sit in my kitchen, staring out the window, a word recurs, an idea, insisting itself upon the situation: remoteness. I moved to Big Sky country to get it. As an angler reflecting upon the fabric of American sport afield, I recognized the essential thread to be a romance with far places. In short, I'd identified the Mainstream and wanted in.

My early fishing days were spent in a northern California cabin snuggled against the hillside beneath stands of redwood. Fishing was more plain and intimate then, and the invocation "Take a boy fishing!" required but a few Bass-O-Renos and perhaps a small outboard motor, called a "kicker," for immediate implementation. On a bookshelf beside our cabin's fireplace was a pile of old magazines, sporting journals mostly, and some outdated tackle catalogues. This collection of allusions was rife with visions of adventure in which the canoe loomed large as a vehicle of escape. A guide, invariably of French descent and dressed appropriately in a red-and-black-checked wool shirt, took us to lakes and rivers teeming with unusually large brook trout or northern pike somewhere in the vastness of the Canadian outback. *Portage!* How much more a vision of unsoiled landscape this word promised than, say, *ecology.*

But before I founder completely in fatuous recall, it occurs to me that until very recently, among the hundred thousand–odd words placed by the *Oxford Unabridged* at my disposal, the adjective least correct to describe my own angling past is *remote.*

SAN FRANCISCO BAY:   It is four-thirty in the morning on June 21, 1966. I am later than planned because of the time it took to clear myself with the policeman who pulled me over in San Anselmo for "suspicious behavior." Was it the generally fishy odor about the car which, in the end, convinced the law of my salient innocence? I don't know. In any case, we parted amicably.

Now I am parking the car near a maintenance station on the Marin County end of the Richmond–San Rafael Bridge. I expect to be joined soon by an acquaintance but since he hasn't arrived I decide to walk out to the bridge itself for a quick preview. On the way, rats scurry for cover behind a shabby row of shrubs. These would not be your large Norways, the kind you might see in the tropics sitting boldly in a palm while you sip your rum and tonic on the veranda below. No, the pusillanimous little rodents that people my morning are inclined to cower behind slimy rocks near the freeway, struggling on an equal footing with Marfak for control of the last strands of seaweed, or waiting in crevices for the next colloidal high tide.

I brush past the *Pedestrians Prohibited* sign, jump the low guardrail, and trot to the second lightpost. There is no visible traffic but from the north I hear a diesel truck shift down just before the crest that will bring him into view and then onto the bridge approach. He will be doing seventy when he reaches me so I hook one leg over the railing, grip the light standard, and try to become inconspicuous. I would rather not be sucked under the rear wheels of a truck and trailer full of rutabagas. He goes by with a blast and the bridge vibrates ominously as I watch his lights fade toward Richmond.

I run out to the next light and look down. As I'd hoped, half a dozen dark forms are finning in the shadow beneath the bridge. I am especially excited by the largest, which is a striped bass of at least thirty pounds. To my right, a pod of smelt moves nearby on a tangent certain to prompt an attack. The little fish are attracted by the brilliant light overhead. In their lack of purpose they seem ephemeral, like a translucent curtain quivering near a window, while the heavy predators lurking in the dark are deliberate and potent. In a moment the black shapes explode outward, sending the smelt arcing away in a shower of flashing bodies.

Satisfied, I turn back toward the approach in time to see the California Highway Patrol car coming at me, its nose down under heavy braking.

"What are you doing out here, buddy?"

"Going fishing soon as it's legal time."

"Is that your car parked back at the maintenance building?"

"Yes."

"Well, it's illegally parked. Better move it. Now get going and don't walk out here anymore."

On my way to the car I see the patrolman who'd questioned me get out and look over the railing. Then the amber light is flashing and the driver is out too. Together they lean over the side, pointing.

I see Frank's blue sedan come down the exit ramp and turn south. When I reach him he is untying his boat and I begin to do the same. In a few seconds we will have them in the water. In order to launch we must trespass. The land belongs to the State of California, and although I've never been verbally warned off, any number of *Keep Out* signs are posted.

For about eight years I kept a boat chained and locked behind a large sign reading *Cable Crossing*. Once a year the sign would be repainted, and white paint would get on the chain. Some yards away in a square blockhouse belonging to San Quentin Penitentiary, trustees worked during the day. Each season they planted a handsome little vegetable garden which I was careful never to disturb. I often talked to one convict in particular after fishing. It would take some minutes to put the boat behind the sign and then carry everything else up to the car. He would call a greeting and I'd perhaps comment on the progress in the garden. Then he'd ask, always rather plaintively, about the fishing. He said he'd liked to go fishing before he got "inside."

One December we had a severe storm, accompanied by especially high tides. Afterward, I went over to check the boat and all that was left was the chain. I was poking around the beach when I heard my friend's voice.

"Looking for your boat?"

"Guess it's gone," I replied sadly.

"No, I saw it break loose and caught it. Then I dragged it up there," he said. "Only thing I couldn't find was the seat." Beyond the garden I could see the trim little El Toro upside down on a pair of two-by-fours.

In recent years there have been no inmates at the blockhouse and the garden lies fallow beneath wild anise. In a sense this has meant more license to trespass but I stopped keeping a boat behind the sign when I knew there would be no trustees to look after it.

Back at the launch, it is a windless, overcast morning. Sunrise is due in an hour but the eastern horizon over San Pablo Bay is still dark. Bursts of flame glow against a cloudy ceiling above Point Molate, tangible evidence that behind the latter's headlands lies the Standard Oil Company of California's research center. Its sprawl of cylinders, cones, and rectangles is petroleum's bitter ode to the cubists. At Point San Quentin, the flaring fires have become a familiar greeting, like the dew on a chokecherry bush that starts off the trout fisherman's day in the Rockies.

"Did you look?" Frank asks.

"They're there."

We row around the tilted bow of a derelict tugboat, then past rotted pilings left from the ferryboat days. Over on the approach a yellow bridge-patrol truck moves slowly, flashing its warning lights. Switching on a spotlight, the driver scans the water, catching sight of Frank and me. Then the light is off and the truck starts toward the toll plaza. Unseen overhead, a black-crowned nighthawk rasps its singularly forlorn call. The smell of an institutional breakfast wafts unappetizingly across the water from San Quentin, an odor not unlike that of a cow barn in winter. No croissants and chilled grapefruit sections this morning, to be sure.

There is a fast tide and we must row smartly to pass beneath the bridge, where it is always dank and dripping. Sounds are magnified and echoed, especially the wavelets slapping against pilings. Reflected light plays on the girders overhead, and just before we emerge I see several bass hovering at the edge. Frank rows into the dark while I decide to try a few casts at the first light. The piling directly beneath the lamp attracts my attention so I drop the large bucktail fly where the current will swing it into the shadows.

Instantly there is a take and I set the hook twice. This is always the moment when I wonder if the bass will go under the bridge and break off on a sharp barnacle. But I've learned that initial light pressure generally encourages them to dive toward the boat. Now my bass pulls around into the dark, and I try to gauge its size. It is a stubborn fish that resolutely resists all the strain I can manage on a fifteen-pound tippet. Eventually I land it and estimate a weight slightly above twenty pounds. Frank is anchored under the third light, where I see angular splashes as fish erupt under a school of bait.

Walt Mullen showed me the bridge and how to fish it. When we first met, shortly after it was built, I was sixteen and he was more than eighty. Walt had taken my father fishing and hunting back in the twenties when my dad was going to Stanford.

Mullen was an old sign painter, wiry and spry, surely no more than a hundred pounds soaking wet. I wanted to learn the sign business so I hung around his shop. Because my patience proved short and my business acumen entirely nonexistent, we always ended up talking about fishing. He loved it more than anyone I'd ever met. In the front pocket of his coveralls he always had a tide book, dog-eared and paint-smeared.

"See here," he said one day, pointing out the numerals. "There's a good tide in three days. If the water's clear and it's not too windy, I'll take you out to the bridge."

At that point my own experience was primarily academic insofar as fly-casting for striped bass was concerned. Walt didn't fly-fish but he knew instinctively I would catch fish on the streamers I showed him. I'd read about certain pioneer anglers on the East Coast who caught striped bass by fly-fishing. I knew also that Joe Brooks, the noted Virginian, was much interested in stripers and had caught one of twenty-nine pounds, six ounces in 1948 out of Coos Bay, Oregon. This fish was the acknowledged fly-rod record.

For several years Walt and I fished together regularly, until I married and became too busy and he closed his shop, moving the business to another county. Occasionally I'd see him at the bridge. His eyes were failing and he didn't trust himself in a boat anymore, so he'd cast from the rocks, often a futile gesture since fish rarely fed close to shore.

One windy, choppy evening Bill Schaadt and I were in our boat at the third light.

"Look." Bill pointed.

On the bridge, hunched against the railing, oblivious to speeding traffic and thoroughly unable to distinguish Bill or me, was Walt clutching an enormous spinning rod. Cocking it back, he used it to drive his lure in a trajectory which carried it over a school of bass I'm sure he never saw. His face was locked in an expression of determination that did not make him look any less like an angling Ichabod Crane.

"Boy," Bill said, "now there's a guy who likes to fish!" As we'd hoped and anticipated, Walt hooked a striper, stalked grimly back to the rocks, and landed it.

Several years passed during which I did not see Walt Mullen. Then one cold spring morning I was out at the bridge alone. To avoid the noisome mob of trollers, with whom the bridge had become a favorite haunt, I'd begun going at odd hours and poorish tides. When it grew light I saw a figure on the rocks, casting. Walt! I drew up my anchor and rowed in, circling widely so I wouldn't spoil anything. Close in, I turned but could no longer see anyone.

I went ashore and called out, but got no response. I looked under the bridge and finally crossed the freeway to search the other side. There was no one. I felt a deep sense of loss, an uneasy melancholy. I went home.

Later I found out Walt had died earlier that spring.

I row around behind Frank. The bass are there and I see the heavy swirls as they feed. Traffic on the bridge is picking up, early commuters. They are too low in their cars to see us but the truck drivers give a wave or short blast of the horn. It is getting light, a gray dawn that I imagine could be heavily depressing to a man facing eight hours on the production line.

"The coldest winter I ever spent," wrote someone, "was a summer in San Francisco." I wonder momentarily if this, in part, explains the high suicide rate and high alcohol intake for which the City on the Bay is known. Frank and I are virtually within sight of well over a million people, yet alone. We are perhaps out of step, ill-placed and ill-timed, in a sphere where cogs must mesh and all parts syncopate to keep the system running smoothly. Even within the framework of angling as a popular endeavor, our methods are archaic: fly-rods and rowboats. But we are touching something unrestricted, wild and arcane, beyond the reach of those who carefully maintain one-dimensional lives. I know there are people in the city nearby whose one contact today with unreconstructed nature will be to step in a diminutive pile of poodle excrement.

When I looked into the mirror during the late fifties I saw a striped-bass fisherman who often imagined, wrongly, that he was doing something remarkable and unique.

At the time an old gent by the name of Ellis Springer was pier keeper for the Marin Rod and Gun Club, which was situated only a few feet from the bridge. He let me use the club's launching ramp, dock, and fish-cleaning table even though I was not a member.

Ellis was never seen without a light-blue captain's hat and stubby cigar. He talked often of the days he'd spent in the Spanish-American War but his manner of speech was so unique that you could understand nothing of what he said. I didn't think he knew what fly-fishing was, and wanting to let him in on my little discovery, I gave a demonstration one day off the dock. He looked properly astonished and when I showed him my flies, he became incoherently excited, exclaiming, "Yeeehhh! Hoopty poopty! Hoopty poopty!"

These exclamations became a permanent part of all subsequent conversations.

"Hi, Springer."

"Eeeeehhh! Hoopty poopty!"

I used to carry fish around in the back of my car the way other kids my age carried a six-pack of Country Club. I'd show Ellis and he'd become truly frantic.

"Yeeeehhh! Hoopty poopty! Hoopty poopty!"

Gradually I became aware of the fact he called everything that was not strictly a sardine fillet a hoopty poopty.

Frank hooks a bass. I put my anchor down out of his way but still close enough to reach the school. I see two powerful boils and cast the bulky fly on a slow loop toward the swirl closest to a piling. I overshoot so the fly tinks against the bridge, hanging momentarily between the rail and roadway. As it flutters downward I see the number 9 stenciled above on an abutment.

The take is authoritative and my response lifts the clearly visible fly line from the water, curving it abruptly to the left as a sheet of droplets limns the fish's first long run. It is not a frenetic contest as the striper stays deep, far from the boat. But I am not inclined to carry out these contests gently and soon have the fish nearby. Once, glowering, he shoots away beneath a crescent of spray only to be turned in a vertical wallow. After all, nothing in their lives really prepares fish to deal with the relentless ordeal of being hooked. Walt Mullen described playing a fish by saying, "then it fooled around and fooled around." And that is exactly it.

In the boat the fish is big.

"It's more than twenty-five," I say to Frank.

Earlier we had discussed a twenty-five-pound striper caught accidentally by a fly-fisherman in the Russian River. It seemed more appropriate that a fish taken by design should receive top honors for the season. Naturally, we both expressed the hope that one of us would catch such a fish. Now, back at the beach, we lay three large bass in front of the *Cable Crossing* sign.

"That one's bigger than the thirty-pounder I caught last season," says Frank. He takes a Polaroid of me holding the fish, and a minute later the image appears, looking distant and journalistic. After I promise to call him as soon as I get the thing weighed, I head for San Rafael and Frank goes off to work in San Francisco.

Later, I call.

"It's big, isn't it?" Frank asks right away. "I've been looking at this snapshot all morning."

"Yes. Thirty-six pounds, six ounces."

The record Joe Brooks had held for eighteen years was broken. When I got to know Joe he would always introduce me as "a great salt-water fisherman," which was embarrassing because while he was alive he was so clearly the greatest. Now others have caught bigger bass, eliminating my personal stake in the matter. It is a relief to be reminded that competition in angling is entirely beside the point and that I'm simply an angler of average persuasion and ability who happened to cast a fly near a large, hungry fish one morning. Besides, there are too many other things to think about, like a certain broad shovel on the porch. I finished all the Jack Daniels last night and this morning I am hopelessly snowed in.

# 22

# Striped Bass and Southern Solitude

Ellington White

S triped bass fishing can be as social or as solitary an experience as an
individual wishes to make it. For much of the season, most well-
known striper fishing locations may be laden with anglers. But there are
countless other reaches of shoreline that offer cooperative bass to those who
cherish more private encounters. In Striped Bass and Southern Solitude
(1966), Ellington White imparts a quiet wisdom won in pursuing striped
bass, alone, in the backwaters of Chesapeake Bay.

---

The best way to fish is alone. The best time to fish is the fall. Believing
these simple truths to be self-evident, I set out alone each fall to fish
the rivers and creeks that flow out of Virginia into the Chesapeake
Bay. It is a good time of year all around. Everybody else in the world
is watching a football game. Leaves cover the roadside beer cans, and
the traffic is light. Whenever a car appears pulling a boat, I know it is
bound for the city, not the sea, for the water skiers have beached their
skis and skin divers have taken up bowling. Praise the fall.

In truth, fishermen should do as fish do in the summer—lie low.
We should give the beaches to the sunbathers and admit that during

this idle season, when the great fiber-glass fleet rules the waterways, the thing to do is haul in our lines and run for cover. Of course, we will never do this. We aren't as smart as fish. We persist in thinking that the summer is big enough for all of us—fishermen, skin divers, water skiers, the whole shebang. What a delusion.

But now it is the fall, and I am driving east on Route 33. Pine trees crowd the shoulders, and the morning sun is hot. In the Tidewater, summer and fall merge with each other so quietly that for a few weeks you need a calendar to tell where you are. Straddling two seasons, one foot in each, you feel both seasons at once.

At West Point, under a cloud of pulpmill smoke, I cross the Pamunkey and Mattaponi rivers, tributaries of the York River, which enters the bay just north of the James. All of these rivers belong to the fall in my mind, the James especially, where I once saw the fall arrive.

I had taken a boat up the river to fish for bass in the mouth of a small creek near Presque Isle Swamp, about twelve miles below Richmond. Here the James takes its time, dawdling along between odorous mud flats, mesmerizing fish and fishermen alike. It just about put me to sleep that day, I recall. After several hours I had had enough, and started back, half paddling, half drifting down the river on the outgoing tide, drowsing among the slumberous sounds of wallowing carp and turtles dropping off logs.

It was a warm day in early October. Most of the clothing I had started out in lay heaped in the bottom of the boat. I was glad the tide and I were going the same way. Farther down the river a handful of gulls was circling a row of stakes that had once supported fish-nets. The shoreline slid past, marshy and still. I drifted by a small bay and across a gravel bar. By this time the gulls were wheeling overhead. The fog lifted just enough for me to catch the glimmerings of an idea, something about gulls following stripers. . . .Oh, nonsense, I thought. Nevertheless, there was the rod resting against the middle seat. All I had to do was pick it up. Why not? I cast into the shore. It was an idle cast and went farther than I had intended it to, landing among a drift of leaves and pine needles. The surface plug bobbed a few times. The leaves bulged and then blew open. It was an astonishing moment. I had often driven hundreds of miles chasing stripers up and down the eastern seaboard, and here I had *drifted* into a school of them. Later I visualized our paths as two crooked lines, wobbling all over the river, and somehow miraculously bisecting under a flock of gulls. In ten minutes it was all over. We had drifted apart, and without a motor I had no way of following them. It didn't matter, though. I had four of them, all about six pounds, flopping on top of my clothes.

I don't know of any fish that gives as much pleasure to as many fishermen as the ubiquitous striper. He may not be as dazzling as a bonefish or as much a roughneck as a snook, but he covers more ground than these fish do and so comes into contact with more people. There is nothing provincial about him, either. He can get along in fresh water just as well as he can in salt water, river water as well as ocean water, shallow water or deep water—it's all the same to him. People fish for him in boats, on banks, in the surf or by wading. They use trolling rods, boat rods, casting rods, spinning rods, fly rods and every kind of bit made—wood, plastic, feathered and live. And he survives them all. Praise the striper, I thought, looking at my four, the most democratic fish that swims.

By the time I reached the landing, the temperature had dropped sharply. A chill wind swept across the river. I climbed back into my clothes and walked home smelling of fish. That was six years ago. The sweater is still with me, as is the scent. Maybe nobody else can smell it, after tons of mothballs and innumerable dry cleanings, but I was putting the sweater in the car this morning, prior to setting off down Route 33, and caught a whiff of it again, every bit as strong as that day I passed through a school of stripers.

Stutts Creek, my destination, is one of many tidal creeks found along the Virginia side of the Chesapeake Bay. Itself a branch of the bay, it sprouts still other branches and ends up looking on a map like a tree that has fallen into the bay's marshy fringes. Once a waterway for crabbers and oystermen, it has become in recent years something of a playground as well, conveying many more svelte Chris-Crafts than lumbering workboats. But like playgrounds everywhere, it is crowded in the summer and all but empty during the winter.

When I fish Stutts Creek I always stay with a man who was raised on it, Norris Richardson, who runs Pine Hall, an inn for fishermen and exhausted city dwellers who drive down on the weekends from Richmond. Pine Hall is a large white house overlooking the creek from a summit of green grass. Norris runs the place as though he were not really trying to, and as a result it is one of the best-run places I know of. You have the comfortable feeling that everyone is there to relax, even the help. Norris is a small, distracted man with an inexhaustible supply of country stories, little pastoral romances about coons and possums and what happened to old Uncle So-and-so when a pail of crabs turned over in his kitchen. Listen to enough of these tales and you forget all about Vietnam and overpopulation. I always like to hear one or two before setting off up the creek. They are like steppingstones to another world.

Stutts Creek enters the bay between two islands lying just off the mainland. One of these, Gwynn Island, is a well-known vacation spot, but the other, Rigby Island, is little more than an exposed sandbar. There is a channel between the islands, but elsewhere the water is shallow and marshy.

Stripers seem to regard the bay as a school they have to complete before graduating into the Atlantic Ocean. The school lasts four years. A few dropouts may tackle the ocean sooner than that, but the majority are content to wait until graduation day. Then they are ready to join the big ocean community on the outside. At least, this is what a tagging program instigated by the Atlantic States Marine Fisheries Commission indicates. The young striper just out of school tends to stay pretty close to home for the first year or so, but as his size increases so does his boldness, and off he goes to prowl the New England coast 700 miles away. In the fall he frequently returns, packing weights of twenty and thirty pounds. It is a curious fact that stripers reach the bay about the same time that alumni are arriving in Charlottesville, Virginia, to watch Mr. Jefferson's eleven take another licking, but if you think *that* homecoming is worth watching you ought to see what happens when the Old Boys get together in the bay. It's an alumni secretary's dream. Gulls throw up tents all over the place, covering the big feeds, and the campus becomes one huge thrashing contest. Before long the racket reaches the shore, and here comes a fleet of fishermen pounding out to join in the fun.

It's a great sport if you like that sort of thing, and most striper fishermen do, but not caring for homecomings myself, in Charlottesville or the bay, I cut the motor and drift into the shallows behind Rigby Island. It's quieter there. You can hear the tide running through the grass. I toss out the anchor, rig up a rod, stuff my pockets with flies, climb into a pair of boots and wade off in search of a few first-graders.

Cold nights have distilled the water. Croakers, spot, crabs, nettles—all of summer's impedimenta—have been frozen out, and the once-green marsh is now the color of bronze. A line of pine trees stands on the far shore; nearer, dead limbs mark an oyster bed. Where the bay has breached Rigby Island slightly left of center, the tide crosses a sandbar and then spreads out over the marsh, dividing it into a number of small grassy clumps. The water is a hard, glinty, blue.

I have never yet caught a fish on a first cast, nor have I ever made a first cast without thinking I would catch a fish. My heart pounds, my hands shake. I tie on a white streamer, wet it with saliva so that it will sink fast, and drop it at the edge of the marsh. It crosses the tide on a series of swift jerks and returns to my feet untouched. I pick it up and cast again. By the fifteenth cast my hands are steady and my heart has resumed its normal tempo. Now begins the long haul.

Stripers like moving water, and when the tide is slack so are they. I walk along casting. Hours pass. I switch to a popping bug and try that until the marsh is brimful of water and a gold chain leads across it to where the sun is settling into a thicket of trees. Lights appear on shore. Gulls are coming in to roost on the channel markers. Soon it will be dark. I want a fish to whack the popper right out of the water, and I hold onto this hope as long as there is light. Then, when there is no more light, I return to Pine Hall.

So begins the first of many fall weekends on Stutts Creek. As the days shorten, my clothes increase. Sweaters pile up. By December I look like a woolen balloon with legs. Norris Richardson's dogs jump aside when they see me coming. Some mornings dawn fair, others overcast and wet. The best mornings are those when frost covers the ground and a brittle stillness films the creek. Coming up, the sun looks like a forest fire. The worst mornings come out of Canada on a northwest wind that wants to shred you alive, and you need more than sweaters to keep warm. Some fishermen use insulated underwear, some carry bottles, some turn on the furnace words of the English language. I resort to fantasy myself. As soon as numbness reaches the top of my waders, I wrap myself in the vision of a big striper who has gotten tired of homecoming and returned to the shallows of his youth. I see him passing through the inlet just as I am rounding the marsh directly in front of him. There was a time when he would not enter the shallows without company, but now that he has grown up the rewards of fellowship have diminished and he finds that the marsh is something of a relief after the tumult of the bay. So here he is enjoying the freedom of being alone, and here I am doing the same—smothered in wool, walking toward him. I see him nudge the grass. His tail lifts a cloud of sand, then carries him into the mouth of a small feeder creek. (In actual fact, there is such a creek, though it lies closer to Pine Hall than it does in my fantasy. I never pass it without thinking what a wonderful place it would be to catch a striper—smooth sandy bottom, tufts of grass choking the mouth, a line of pine trees to break the wind.) Once he is in the creek, however, the striper finds that the water is not as deep as it appeared to be on the outside and he starts back, cruising like a porpoise. By then I have planted a popper squarely in the middle of the opening, and when he is within sight of it I twitch the line and the popper jumps forward. You can guess the rest.

It is astonishing how much heat a scene like that can generate.

For a moment last Thanksgiving Day I thought I had caught this fish. I went out early in the morning and fished straight through until dusk. It was a cold, blustery day. The wind piled up big waves and hurled them at the shore. Casting a heavy saltwater fly rod is hard work in itself, but casting it in the wind for seven or eight hours is pure torture. In the middle of the afternoon I found three small fish, two- and three-pounders, huddled up in a pocket of deep water, but catching them had rekindled no fires, and by evening I was numb and sore all over.

Even my fantasy had quit working. The tide had just about run itself out, and so had I. I switched to a spinning rod, a less taxing instrument than a fly rod, and waded out along a point of land for a few final casts. I tossed the lure, a weighted jig, into a trench the tide had dug between two sandbars. It was an ordinary sort of place, a place you fish because you know you should rather than because it appeals to you. I had fished the place many times before, ever since Brook Jones, a fine fisherman from Richmond, had pointed it out to me. Brook takes fish out of it all the time, but I had never had much luck with it. Today was different. The lure bounced down one wall of the trench, disappeared in deep water, then climbed up the other wall. It had just reached the top when a shadow rose off the bottom and pulled it back down. I knew it was a big fish by the size of the shadow. He lunged around in the depths for a while, then plowed off across the shallows with a second fish right behind him. Why the second fish, I don't know. Perhaps the two of them had been lying in the trench getting fat together. In any case, the follower soon veered off in the direction of the channel while my fish bore straight ahead. There is nothing spectacular about the way stripers behave after they are hooked. A heavy fish simply lays into a line and bulls his way along. He's a plodder. I could have let this striper run a mile before he reached anything to break off on, but it had been a long cold day and I was taking no chances. I could plod, too. So I set a hard drag and in time wore him down the way you break horses—with sheer force.

One thing he had done was thaw me out. I could feel again. He would go eight or nine pounds, I supposed. Holding him up against the horizon, I found there was more light left in him than was left in all the sky—no fantasy fish, but a good solid striper, all the same.

*The unseen quarry and mysterious dark water, the pleasure taken in the strong and skillful cast, the sound and smell of sea and weather, the healing solitude, and the suspense, are reward enough to the true sportsman who seeks no profit from his hobby, and surfcasting for striped bass probably claims more fanatics than any other form of saltwater fishing.*

—PETER MATTHIESSEN,
*Men's Lives,* 1986

# 23

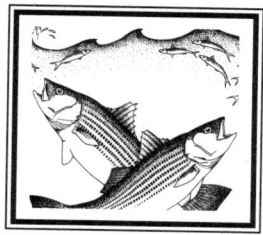

# Season's End

*John Cole*

J n late autumn, schools of striped bass sweep the surf of eastern Long
Island as they migrate southward. For decades, seiners worked these
waters for stripers and other fishes, gunning their dories through the breakers to lay a long arc of net to be hauled to the beach. To better their odds
before making a set, baymen would ride the sands in their trucks and
search for signs of bass. One day John Cole and the rest of his haul seine
crew observed a rare and savage scene, a blitz in which striped bass were
prey rather than predator, described in Striper: A Story of Fish and Man.

---

I stare out to sea, at the far horizon. Inshore, the ocean is calmed by
the wind off the land. The waves are sharp, curling, and the northerly
gale blows mare's tails of spume off the crests as they move toward
the beach. But on the far horizon, where the wind reaches beyond
the lee, the seas build and cut a jagged pattern along the line where
water meets the sky. I try to preoccupy my thoughts with the oddness
of the seascape created by the wind offshore. The horizon jumps, vibrates, and I watch it, imagining what it must be like out there in a
small boat bucking the chop and the freezing spray.

Dark clouds roll like cannonballs across the sky; they are the leading edge of a cold front, sweeping down from the north, pushing winter before it. More fat flakes of snow slant across the dunes, the sand hisses against the side of the dory; I can feel the twine stiffening in my hands as the windchill freezes the sea-soaked netting where it lies on the beach. In the afternoon light of the short day, the seawater turns green, splotched white with its offshore waves—a white made starker by the gunmetal sky and the hurtling snow.

I wonder to myself if what I see can be birds, or a snow patch, whirling in its own tight orbit far beyond the bar. In the snow it is difficult to tell. Then, as they move closer, the birds emerge, tossing and turning in a white cluster like the snowflakes, but with a focus to their churning. They are edging, bit by bit, toward the shore, and as they come nearer I can see white water at the bottom of their funnel-shaped flock. They are gulls and gannets, and they are working over fish. There can be no doubt now about that. This is a sure sign, the finest kind of sign.

"Hey, look there! Look there!" I yell. I find a freedom in the rush, a setting to rights in the fact of the birds. It is a signal that fish are there as certain as any I could have spotted. Ted looks, and he yells too.

"That's a bunch, that's sure. That's a bunch. Looks like they're moving inshore too." He begins trotting to the truck, his waders thumping as he moves. "Come on, boys. Come on, get that twine in the dory. Jesus, Johnny, get moving, will you."

Peter whoops and grins. Together we hustle in the last of the seine. Ted starts the truck, pulls the rig along the beach a bit, closer to the fish. They are still too far offshore to be reached, but they are on top, moving in.

Their activity is frantic. The green sea is frothed with constant splashing. I see geysers of breaking water spout aloft, to be atomized by the wind. I have never seen such large gouts of foam in a school of bass before. These are, I decide, either very large bass, or else the school is feeding on a different sort of cold water bait. There is an aura of panic to the scene that I have never before witnessed.

"Something is driving those bass," Ted yells. He is standing on top of the truck cab, looking out to sea. "Them fish ain't feeding. Something is feeding on them." Ted takes off his long-billed cap. His silver-white hair, close-cropped, stands out against his tanned face.

He holds his arm with the cap in his hand to shield his eyes from the wind and snow. "Them's porpoise, that's what they are. That's what's going on out there. Them porpoise are driving those bass. God dammit, there's no telling what will happen, goddamn porpoise."

I can see them now—black fins rising from curved black backs, sliding from under the green sea, sleek, surging, pushing aside the water in wedged welts of white foam. And in front of the wedges, the bass scatter, flashing, panicking like minnows before the assault of the torpedoing scores of porpoise. I am stunned by the scale of the slaughter. There must be a hundred or more porpoise, a vast school. Like wolves running down a pack of lambs, they are herding the small bass, this way, then that way, but always toward the beach where the stripers will have to leap to the sand if they are to find sanctuary from these predators.

The entire mass, hunters and hunted, moves into the surf line. We can hear the splashing now. We can hear the explosive whoosh of air from the porpoise blowholes when they surface. The bass are practically at our feet. The regular pattern of the waves is set asunder by the turmoil at the ocean's edge. The porpoise look huge to me— great black hulks, roaring like locomotives along the walls of the waves.

One breaches in the wash. His entire twelve-foot length comes free of the surf in a great leap that takes the creature from its element, from the green and white sea, and pinions it against the cannonball clouds of this winter sky. The porpoise underside is ivory white, a curving bib beneath its jaws. And there, caught across those jaws is a striped bass at the moment of its doom. The porpoise teeth close. Incredibly, the creature is still aloft against my horizon like a demon come alive. Bright bass blood spills along the ivory bib, red against the cream.

The porpoise falls back into the sea; foam fountains against the skyline; the porpoise and its fellows are once again curving black backs beneath the waves. The leaping creature no longer hangs against the sky, yet hangs forever in my memory.

The school of bass turns offshore now. Having found no sanctuary in the surf, the frenzied fish once again make for deeper water— anything to get shed of their tormentors. I can see that we, too, are doomed.

"They're getting away. They're moving out." I am desperate. "Ted, Ted, come on, let's set, let's go."

"No, Johnny, no." Ted shakes his head. Like me, he must be wondering what stars have crossed this day. "We can't set around them porpoise. They'll tear the seine to shreds. Besides, the bass are moving too fast. They'll never sit still long enough for us to set around them, not being chased like that. Ted watches as the patch of white water, the black backs and the funnel of birds moves southwest, across the outer bar. "We might as well give it up. Porpoise moving along the beach like that, there ain't going to be a bass inshore between here and Shinnecock."

So this is how a season ends, with the four of us, sitting on the dory, or in the truck, watching as the last school we'll see till spring is pursued by the marauders who have stolen what was to be our Christmas haul, the twenty boxes of money fish that would have put cash in my pockets, paid some of my bills.

Snow comes harder now, blowing flat, straight across the beach. The wind is picking up; I can hear the sand hissing more steadily against the dory's windward side. The sky has grown blacker, the sea green, feathered with building whitecaps. The working birds are as difficult to distinguish from the snow as they were when I first saw them, when this entire melodrama began. God damn, why, why couldn't we have had just one break, just this one haul?

*The first run of a striped bass is likely to be a long one and a strong one, and if sizeable fish are about, it is well to have a well-filled reel.*

—LESLIE P. THOMPSON,
*Fishing in New England,* 1955

# 24

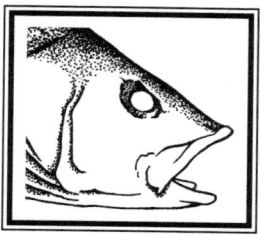

# Last Moon

## Al Reinfelder

T he dedication of the hard-core surfcaster is without match among fishermen. These anglers inhabit a harsh and elemental world of pitched waves, swift riptides, rugged terrain, sleepless nights, and often, long interludes between willing fish. Nonetheless, many surfcasters cannot get their fill, fishing the fall run beyond its days and nights of plenty, all the way to its withering conclusion. In Last Moon (1971), Al Reinfelder bids a brief farewell to another season in the surf.

---

Tonight, if it is clear, an icy white circle will drift amongst the tangled treetop branches hung randomly with tattered leaves. It is the moon of December, the first moon of winter, the last moon of the year.

As this moon wanes into the blackness of mid-month, days will be no more than extended afternoons. The sun is small now, and close to the earth—even at noon. The end of the season comes.

Somewhere along Gin Beach a lone buggy will glide along the hard sands toward Shagwong Point. From habit, the rider will scan the scudding wave tops, watch the high-gliding gulls scan the seas, listen to the wind. But he may not see very much of diving birds and foaming breaks of fish. Out on the long, deep reef, some bait will still be moving toward the point. At times, tight masses of striped bass will spill up unto the twenty-foot waters from the deeper paths from the north. The high gulls will swoop and twist above them. Some bait will entice them to drop into the water, with sharp beaks open and eager. A few boats will drift down from uptide the school and drop diamond jigs into the frosty-green water. Winter bass will take the silver lures as they dart through the ebb.

The loneliness of the surfcaster will wax as the moon wanes; flood as the tide ebbs; and rise as the sun sinks among the purple hills behind him. The wind has blown away all but the faintest traces of tracks at the point. Black kelp, skate eggs, rusty cans, tangled plastic sheets, lie in windrows along the beach. No fish come near the shore.

Numbingly cold outside, the buggy's heater encompasses the fisherman as he watches winter eat into the last days of the year. He nods and heavy fish swarm along the shoreline of his dreams. In the warm summer night his eel, swinging across the tide toward the rocky cluster west of Shagwong Point, is stopped. He raises the surf stick and feels a heavy head shake in surprise and fear out there in the darkest water. Line follows the strong fish as he swims, in yanks and thrusts, out into the current.

Snow swirls crazily outside his window as he awakens from his dozing. No boats are on the reef. He can no longer see the bell and black can. Even the red and black obstruction buoy is lost in whiteness. The caster starts home. Back toward the jetties, south to town, and then west to his home.

Last moon. Season's end.

# 25

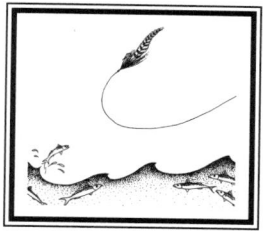

# Striper Moon

### J. Kenney Abrames

W hy *fish for stripers? And if so, why with a strong preference for one particular approach? It is difficult for most anglers to express the deeply personal connection to a favorite species and to the marriage of a fishing technique and specific environment that magnifies and elevates the pursuit. In* Striper Moon *(1994), J. Kenney Abrames deciphers his own enchantment with striped bass, the fly rod, and sand beaches, but with insights that bear on striper fishermen everywhere.*

The fly rod is a graceful lyrical wand. In the hand of a good caster it flows into dance. In the hand of a fisherman its grace extends beyond the cast and penetrates the hidden undulations and rhythms of current. In the hand of an artful fisherman it explores and questions, it gently probes, it speaks a language. Therein lies the grace and beauty of fly rod striper fishing.

In the late sixties I owned a charter boat and fished full time. It was a mixed blessing. I learned a great deal about fishing and fishermen, and that was good. It was fun and the challenge of producing fish for customers kept it interesting. It did have a down side: the routine took over, and the simple joys of fishing disappeared. One day there was one too many dead fish, and I knew my guiding days were over. Since that time a fly rod and a pair of waders have opened up a whole new world of ordinary fishing to me.

Fishing for striped bass has been a part of my life for as long as I can remember. I am grateful that it is. It led me to a love of the ocean and the mysteries it contains. It brought me to appreciate the hidden things that one has to search for to find. It taught me that all life is connected and that time and tide and moon and wind have need of one another.

I seldom fish for stripers from boats. I'm not sure why, I think it has to do with intimacy. There is a quiet measured pace to fishing when you stand in one place and watch the water rise and fall. You begin to notice things you could not see if you were passing by. Walking takes time, but it does not waste it.

There is a type of surf fishing I do that lends itself to this approach so well that to fish the sand beaches any other way is foolish. I have learned through walking that stripers feed in the wash that sweeps up on the sand after the waves break. The water here is so shallow that when the wash from the wave recedes I am standing on dry land. The section of surf inside the break is where I catch my fish. Walking along the beach, looking at the foam and seeing the dorsal fins of stripers cutting through the surface showed me that wading out and trying to fish beyond the waves was not the thing to do.

Walking gives the time you need to see subtle signs that point out where the fish are going to be and how the fish are going to feed. Wade fishing is not better than boat fishing. What it does is force you to commit yourself to a limited fishing area; in a boat you can always sail away to someplace new on a whim, which is not such a bad thing. I grew up in boats and love them but I have learned many things about stripers that I never could have learned if I had not put on my waders and slowed down.

I cannot define striper fishing. The fish lives in so many totally different environments and is fished for successfully with so many methods that definition is beyond me. I do know that the striper is a perfect fly rod fish. He is complex, aggressive and available. He grows to a very large size. He is not easy to catch but not that hard either. He can take you well into your backing or strip your reel if you do not fight him correctly. He will take a tiny shrimp pattern or a foot-long streamer. I have seen him chase down three-pound mackerel faster than the blink of an eye and have watched him tip up and sip half-inch crabs as they floated down in the drift. I have caught him 30 miles offshore on Nantucket Shoals and below a waterfall on the Blackstone River. I have caught him in tidal rivers in the winter and on bathing beaches in the summer. He has personality. He is also a remarkably beautiful fish.

I have always fished for striped bass. My fascination with him has not waned over the years. He has taught me a great deal about fishing, but more often than not he reminds me of the limits of my knowledge. I have fished for many different kinds of fish, often with great effort and desire. I have enjoyed them all. I love salmon and steelhead. It would have been a minor tragedy not to have experienced their rivers and their spirit in my fishing life. Marlin are incredible fish. Giant tuna are simply awe-inspiring. A swordfish is like no other fish that swims. He is a living mystery of the sea. And, I will always fish for stripers.

I have the need to touch mystery. One way I have been able to do this is through the gift and art of fishing. It is a part of my spirit to somehow touch what I know is there but am unable to measure or possess. For these moments of touching I abandon myself and leap into fishing's timeless continuum. Our fishermen's cry of "Just one more cast," can mean many things.

*Ten pounders, twenty pounders, forty pounders, what difference did it make? The roar of Old Ocean, the cries of the gulls, the clean salt smell of seaweed, and the surging rush of a striper on light tackle; those were the things that counted. Those are the things that linger when the season's over and the fish have departed. Those are the things one sees in the dying embers of a fire as a blizzard whines past the frosty windows of your room. Those are the memories one carries to the grave.*

—Van Campen Heilner,
*Salt Water Fishing,* 1937

# Bibliography

"Spring Migration" by John Cole. From *Striper: A Story of Fish and Man,* 1978, 1981. Reprinted by permission of Lyons & Burford Publishers, Inc.

"Fishing in American Waters" by Genio Scott. From *Fishing in American Waters.* New York: Harper and Brothers, 1869.

"In Search of the Striped Bass" by T. Coraghessan Boyle. From *Life,* September 1992. Reprinted by permission of the author.

"Angling for Striped Bass" by Leonard Hulit. From *The Salt Water Angler.* New York: D. Appleton, 1924.

"Forecasting Stripers" by Phil Schwind. From *Cape Cod Fisherman.* Camden, ME: International Marine Publishing Company, 1974. Reprinted by permission.

"Surf Fishing" by Van Campen Heilner and Frank Stick. From *The Call of the Surf.* Garden City, NY.: Doubleday, Page & Co., 1924.

"Night Moves" by Russell Chatham. From *Dark Waters.* Livingston, MT: Clark City Press, 1991. Reprinted by permission of Clark City Press.

"The Hard Business of Surfcasting" by Frank Woolner. From *The Hard Business of Surf Casting,* Vol. 2. New York: Ridge Press and American Broadcasting, 1969. Reprinted by permission.

"Striped Bass" by John Cole. From *Fish of My Years*. Stone Harbor, NJ.: Meadow Run Press, 1995. Reprinted by permission of Meadow Run Press.

"Gold Medal Fish and Others" by Van Campen Heilner and Frank Stick. From *The Call of the Surf*. Garden City, NY.: Doubleday, Page & Co., 1924.

"The Shining Tides" by Win Brooks. *The Shining Tides*. New York: William Morrow, 1952. Reprinted by permission.

"Slaughter at Pochet Hole" by Frank Daignault. From *The Garcia Fishing Annual*, 1976. Reprinted by permission of the author.

"The Surf" by Russell Chatham. From *Striped Bass on the Fly: A Guide to California Waters*. San Francisco: Examiner Special Projects, 1977. Reprinted by permission of Clark City Press.

"Shallow Water Stripers" by Phil Schwind. From *Cape Cod Fisherman*. Camden, ME: International Marine Publishing Company, 1974. Reprinted by permission.

"Hudson River Portraits" by John Bryan. From *Gray's Sporting Journal*, winter 1993. Reprinted by permission of *Gray's Sporting Journal*.

"The Joys of Fishing" by Emmett Gowen. From *The Joys of Fishing*. Chicago: Rand McNally, 1961. Reprinted by permission.

"On Urban Shores" by Ian Frazier. First appeared in *The New Yorker*, 10 January 1994. Reprinted by permission of the author.

"Growing Up with *Roccus*" by Dan Levin. "Growing up with *Roccus*." From *Yankee* Magazine, September, 1967. Reprinted by permission.

"Menemsha Bight: Bass Derby" by Red Smith. Originally published as "Menemsha Bight Bass Derby" in *Red Smith on Fishing: Around the World*. Garden City, NY.: Doubleday, 1963. Used by permission of Doubleday, a division of Bantam Doubleday Dell Publishing Group, Inc.

"Surf Fishing: The Nighttime Provides an Edge" by Nelson Bryant. From *The New York Times*, 1980. Reprinted by permission of the author.

"No Wind in the Willows" by Russell Chatham. From *Angler's Coast*. Livingston, MT: Clark City Press. Reprinted by permission of Clark City Press.

"Striped Bass and Southern Solitude" by Ellington White. From *Sports Illustrated*, 10 October 1966. Reprinted by permission of the author.

"Season's End" by John Cole. From *Striper: A Story of Fish and Man*, 1978, 1981. Reprinted by permission of Lyons & Burford Publishers, Inc.

"Last Moon" by Al Reinfelder. From *The Long Island Fisherman*, 2 December 1971. Reprinted by permission of *The Long Island Fisherman*.

"Striper Moon" by J. Kenney Abrames. From *Striper Moon*. Portland, OR: Frank Amato Publications, 1994. Reprinted by permission of Frank Amato Publications.